PROTECTED AWAKENINGS

Opening your heart to guidance and synchronicities

JESSICA TRIAS

WOW Book Publishing™

First Edition Published by Jessica Trias

Copyright © 2022 Jessica Trias

WOW Book Publishing™

All rights reserved. Neither this book, nor any parts within it may be sold or reproduced in any form without permission.

No part of this book may be reproduced in any form or by any electronic or mechanical means including information storage and retrieval systems, without permission in writing from the author. The only exception is by a reviewer, who may quote short excerpts in a review.

The purpose of this book is to educate and entertain. The views and opinions expressed in this book are that of the author based on her personal experiences and education. The author does not guarantee that anyone following the techniques, suggestions, ideas or strategies will become successful.

The author shall neither be liable nor responsible for any loss or damage allegedly arising from any information or suggestion in this book.

Dedication

To Sean G Murphy and Ronda Bird Parker.
Without you there would be no awakenings.
Thank you for protecting mine.

Draw close to God,
and God will draw close to you
James 4:8

Contents

Testimonials for *Protected Awakenings* vii
Foreword ix
Acknowledgments xi

Chapter 1. Hidden in a dream 1
Chapter 2. A sound, a feather or a knowing 9
Chapter 3. Your story is your story 17
Chapter 4. Let the universe hold your hand 31
Chapter 5. Several angels fill our world 45
Chapter 6. The Storm 53
Chapter 7. Dressed in White 79
Chapter 8. The angel in my intuition 87
Chapter 9. Surrender to all angels 97
Chapter 10. Angels are Translating 103
Chapter 11. Angel Numbers 111
Chapter 12. The angel I never saw coming 119
Chapter 13. Gratitude Angel 127

Chapter 14. Don't forget the angels..................................139
Chapter 15. Ask the angels to surprise you 147

About the Author 157
Afterword...159

Testimonials for *Protected Awakenings*

"Jessica's story is heart breaking and life changing to make you see that manifesting miracles is always possible"

—**Sean G Murphy**
Texas, United States
International Motivational Speaker
Mentor, Coach, Owner of Metal Profits, Teacher and trainer in Mental toughness
www.SeanGMurphy.com

"A house of miracles in her and in me, awakenings that I never saw in myself"

—**Ronda Bird Parker**
Texas, United States
International Speaker
Christian Entrepreneur
Mentor and Coach

Protected Awakenings

"Jessica speaks from her heart and where she lived and breathed gratitude, it helped her through a major life challenge, and she now has put it to paper. What a strong, positive and powerful soul who believed without a doubt, kept going forward in faith and courage and now is living her dream."

—**Diane Sweeney**
Canada
Retired Nurse
Health Coach Entrepreneur
ca.mannatech.com
International Speaker

Foreword

This book is for anyone who wants to discover more about the invisible support that is always available to them anywhere at any time for any situation.

Jessica shares her heart and captures yours with her unique view of the Universe. You will travel on a journey of your own understanding of spirituality that will surprise you and give you more than you ever expected.

Between these pages you will see synchronicities that add up to the beauty of life with all its twists and turns. With a three-step guide to each chapter, you will see every awakening Jessica has had is only the beginning of a mind shift we all needed.

Vishal Morjaria
UK
Award Winning Author
International Speaker
Teacher and Coach for Wow Book Camp

Acknowledgments

To Jesus Christ, my family and my heart which holds Patricia, Edecio, Jose, Georgie, Oscar and Coco Trias, Rodrigo and all those who have passed, but we have never forgotten. To all my family overseas, Brutus (my tortoise), to Sean again, Ronda and the whole misfit community, thank you for guiding and holding me through such a difficult time. I had no idea what I would get out of. To Danjiela Jukic, Daniela Nunez, Amanda, Anne, Coryn, Dakiya, Diane, Delia, Eugenia, Sebastian, Nikki, Gigi, Vici, Sharon, Lydia, Jayee, Katerin, Keyla, Lio Luis Martinez, Nadine, Rob Cardenas, Erika, Brad Chambers, Jeremy, Steff, Alina, Vach, Wajia, Zalika, Aida, Dana Scranton, Bob Kane, Heather Love, Roz Slade, Rob Smith, Natalia, Jolanta, Pooja, Aria, Christina, Leonardo Wilson, David Poole, Shayne Johnson, Jessica Koop, Karina Keitz, Holly Livingstone, Cristi Stone, Jason Stone, Jason Shay, Step Escobar, Corina Curatola.

All my friends at work, Becky Twiggins, Dani Ross, Dani Long, Sam and Daisy Lowe, Rachel, Emma, Sarah, Adam, Daniel, Olivia, Anona, Tracy, Laura, Lucy Hall, Billie, Samer, Anthony, Morgan, Magda, Megan, Alfie, Becky and James

Protected Awakenings

Salfarlie and everyone I have spent so much time with on poolside. Forgive me If I have missed anyone.

To Nicholas Airewele, Hannah and Sarah Fox, Sammie, Mark Wilberforce, Angie, Holly Scarlett Durkin, I love you so much!

To Mike Katende, Katie Moore, Lauren Ashley, Becky Knight, Sammy Parker, Ellie Bushell, Sarah Jennings, Becci Rees and everyone I ever met at Winchester University.

To all my teachers, people who always inspired me, Gabby Bernstein, Vishal Morjaria, Pauline Barath, Samuel Kitenge, Rhonda Byrne, James Redfield, Bob Procter, Bethany Hamilton, Sarah Young, Natasha Grano, Jackie Minsky, Amanda Marshall, Annie Dalton, Jacqueline Wilson, Geoff Lumley, Sandra and everyone from St. James Church Alperton. If I put you all here I would have another book but I want to say a huge thank you for always encouraging me, from the bottom of my big heart, I love you forever.

CHAPTER 1
Hidden in a dream

On the 15th of April 2010 I sat in bed crying from a dream that had felt so real. I opened my eyes to the sunshine through the window, clutching my duvet in disbelief, I had just had my first dream about my own guardian angel. I knew this from reading up on angels, listening to stories that no one could explain. But this dream felt like a film I hadn't watched before. It was exactly one year since my grandmother had passed away.

I was watching her funeral; my mother was playing the piano and my uncle was sitting in the front row. The whole dream was just like it was in my waking life. As I saw the coffin in the front of the church, I was sitting in the back watching myself sing. I had been singing in church since I was a little girl.

I remember watching my mum sing at church, standing next to her mum Olga, and watching her sing with such purpose and confidence that I didn't see in others in the congregation. The most beautiful harmonies so clearly flowed effortlessly out of her mouth. I had no idea what

Protected Awakenings

they were singing about, but it all felt so beautiful. My other memories in church were of being four years old and sleeping on my granny's chest, waking up to the vicar talking and others telling me to be quiet all the time while my mum was either playing the organ that was loud and scary to me or the keyboard that was softer and meant mummy wasn't that far away. Watching the whole funeral unfold, all the calmness was there, those feelings of a safe place I had as a child came flooding back as I watched my mum play, but this time I wasn't sitting next to granny.

The songs I grew up singing always warmed my heart. But in my dream, I was sitting where there were normally people with their babies next to the door towards the creche. In my dream, as I watched the room, I felt a presence that was undeniable sitting next to me. As I turned to my left, I realised it was my granny. Very shocked now this dream got weird, my granny was next to me, but her coffin was in front of me.

Like a freeze frame in a film, everything slowed down and got quiet. She looked at me and said, "it's over" and I couldn't believe it was her. I was speechless and so confused. She looked at me with wisdom all over her face and it felt so good to hear her voice. Better than when you hear your ex-boyfriend's voice after you have broken up and you miss them more than ever. I still had her phone number saved in my phone even though I never called it. I just wanted to hear her one more time. I watched as they held the coffin high and walked out of the church. When I turned to my left all I saw was empty chairs, and my grandmother Olga, who

Hidden in a dream

was sitting next to me had vanished. I opened my eyes to a wet face, I sat there feeling like I had just come out of the cinema and that was not the ending I expected.

Before you read this book: I want you to study it, be open minded to it and know how important this story is to me. After reading a book called '**How to see your angels**' by Theresa Cheung, I learnt that my granny is my guardian angel and she has always been with me through all my trials and tribulations that I will share with you here. She protected me, spoke to God about me and her prayers keep me alive today.

Please do make notes all over this book, have awakenings, share your findings, and find your spirit guides who want to be connected to you. In this book I want you to connect to what stands out to you and every time you see something you never thought of before I hope you highlight your words or mine.

When I looked up the dream, the words were staring back at me. Apparently when you dream about someone at their own funeral it means that the grieving is over. It was exactly like my granny said and from that day onwards I hand-on-my-heart believe she has always been protecting me.

Grief dreams are very rare, but dreams are very important messages and very underrated. From this dream I not only got a message but only years later realised the power of her prayers and her presence. Dreaming of Olga was a chance to escape the grief I was holding on to, not just mine but for my whole family. I'm grateful I got the chance to hear her and see her one last time, it was the closure I needed and my heart that healed when the pain was stronger than anything I had experienced.

In this book I want to help you connect to your angels, the good guys who had your back all along, the healing angels, the people who have become your family and the universe who holds us and takes away any anxiety that weighs heavily on our hearts. Take this journey with me and change your mindset. Your ancestors are guiding you to be the happy person you really are inside.

I hope you find treasure here like I did, and I hope that you always know that wherever you are, you are protected here and forever.

Maybe you too have had a dream you remember vividly, maybe you have not understood your dreams at all. Maybe you had a nightmare and that scared you and you thought nothing of it. Sometimes there is so much happening in a dream you don't know what it means.

Well, I'm here to say that all your dreams have a hidden meaning behind them. You must follow it as dreams are messages, not something to be afraid of. When I had my dream, I knew it meant something, but only after reading someone else's story, did I realise it was more powerful and held the key to understanding the real pain I was in.

Sometimes we have dreams, and we completely dismiss them. We think that they don't mean anything when they are always guiding us and protecting us from something we could not see in our waking life. Your angels are protecting

Hidden in a dream

you and as they want you to go the right way in life, they also want the highest good for you.

We think that the dreams we have are just our mind running wild. Maybe you just didn't get enough sleep, or you create strange scenarios that look like they don't make sense, this is not true. Every dream has a message. I have helped others to understand their dreams, by looking them up in *The complete A-Z Dictionary of dreams by Ian Wallace* a dream book my mother bought me. Sometimes this alone can unlock the feelings you try to hide in your waking life.

We forget about our dreams and we rush into our waking lives thinking that no one is listening to us when our angels want us to go down the correct path to the blessings that have always been around us.

In this book I have created three steps for each story. I want you to understand the message and connect to it so that you know what to do the next time you're in the lesson that the universe gave you. For example, in this chapter, if you struggle to see what's appearing for you and the hidden messages that may be repeated in a dream. Turn to this chapter and follow my guidance to understand it more.

Protected Lesson - Step 1
Have your own dream journal

Start writing down your messages in your dreams
Grab a notebook and write in it as soon as you wake up from a dream. Write down the date and write everything you

Protected Awakenings

remember, the colours, the words, the visions, whatever was up close and far away. To remember, close your eyes and write what you can.

Sometimes something as simple as a symbol or an animal can tell you exactly the message you need to know.

Make sure you can write in it and put it by your bed so you can pick it up first thing in the morning to remember exactly what you saw. Make it a habit to write down every dream. If you had a dream and you remember it very well, like I did with mine even if it was a long time ago, you can practise remembering what your mind saw at that time. Write it down; everything you noticed and write the date you had the dream in case it's recurring or it connects with another one. That means you must act on that dream straight away by interrupting the lesson or else the lesson will repeat if the lesson is not learnt in your dream or in your waking life.

Protected Lesson - Step 2
What surprised you?

Think about what surprised you the most in the dream. Some people notice hundreds of things in a dream, but one scary thing can be the key. In my dreams I was shocked at how my granny spoke to me. She spoke to me like she had never left me. That's how I knew it was important for her to let me know I was protected by her. When you dream your subconscious goes all over the place. Remember the part of the dream that stands out because it is the compass to what is next or the path of least resistance. Write down how

Hidden in a dream

you felt in the dream and what happened right before you woke up.

Protected Lesson - Step 3
Look up the real meaning

You can type anything into a search engine like this and look up the meaning that speaks to you first out of all of them you find.

Google Search example....

What is the meaning of dreaming of Angels?

Angels are messengers from God they protect us, guide us, or carry out heavenly tasks. Therefore, angel dreams symbolise a greater force that is watching over us, detecting us, or trying to show us something important, which is hidden.

www.chataboutyou.com

Search for any dream meaning like this and look at all the answers for which one stands out to you.

Dream of_____and fill in the blank.

Looking up a dream is very important. As you look up the most surprising thing in a dream be open to all interpretations. As you read you can also start to see what connects to your intuition. Pinpoint what was there and what that word means or that symbol that showed up for you. Was it something that someone said? Was it that you were shocked at what you did that was not like you?

Protected Awakenings

Everything that happened is a message and a missing piece of the puzzle or just your mind wandering after all the thoughts you never let go of before you went to sleep but the more awareness you have the better.

Looking up the meaning of your dream is like listening to your guardian angel. That dream can protect you in another realm in more ways than you will realise.

You are protected even in your dreams, even if they are nightmares and they scare you, they are still messages. So, get a journal. Remember you are the main character, and your angels want you to win. Look up what surprised you and look at the meaning, find the hidden message in the dream and what is the real message and keep interpreting until you pinpoint what it's trying to tell you. Throughout the day it may all come together. Start writing down all your dreams because you never noticed them before. Accept that the message is there and stay open to all ideas as you open your mind and heart to hearing what comes through and what you need to work on for yourself to feel better.

CHAPTER 2
A sound, a feather or a knowing

On the 7th of July 2005, I was in high school going about my normal day at school. A teacher told me to take a note to another teacher and I went on my way to walk to her room. I did as she said, and I took the note to her. When the teacher opened the note, she looked up at me and said, "Are you serious?" Not knowing what she was talking about because I never looked at it - you can tell I'm always miss goody two shoes right? I watched her as she flew to another room, went straight to her phone and started texting frantically. Standing there I had no idea what had happened or the amount of chaos that was happening in London that day. The teacher went to put the TV on, but it was facing away from me, and I couldn't see through the door. The teacher thanked me for the note, so I went back to my class very confused.

At break time my friends were all crying hearing the news spread like wildfire that 56 people had died on a train and 700 people were injured in a terrorist attack in which

Protected Awakenings

explosives had been detonated on two trains and a bus in central London. My father was working there at the time, but thankfully the bus was down the road from his workplace. I did not feel like crying as something in me said he was ok, which he was, and I was so relieved.

Four months on and everyone was terrified of going anywhere. One story that always stayed with me was from one of my friends who said her uncle had been on that train, but he looked up at which direction the train was going in then he noticed he was on the wrong side and heading in the wrong direction. Getting off the train and going towards the other platform he had just gotten off the train that was about to blow up. What he didn't know was that he was following his intuition, a gut feeling, a protection that so many of us have. A feeling of going the wrong way. That inner voice that speaks to you and pulls at you that something is just not right. That voice, that whisper that says no, not that way this way, please listen.

Now that I'm older I have heard stories like this, and I have noticed a reoccurring theme.

When reading books about spirituality, I was learning about so much that was unknown to me. Whenever I have a good idea or I think of something guiding me, I hear my grandmother's wind chime in the garden.

Guardian angels are not just about people and dreams, they can be as simple as a feeling, a noise, a feather or a white light.

A sound, a feather or a knowing

At first, I thought it was just the wind but after I said things to myself like, affirmations or I prayed for something, I would hear it ring whether there was wind or not. Every day we are guided, protected, and held by an invisible presence so pure. This is the real reason we are all alive right now. The prayers your grandparents and great grandparents prayed have reached you today. Your ancestors performed rituals and blessings over you and your path hoping you stay true to yourself. Let the guardian angels follow you wherever you go.

When we have a knowing or we talk about our intuition, sometimes we ignore it. We second guess ourselves. We think that it's a temporary feeling that we have, but our own feeling can save our life and the lives of others. We think that it's just a feeling and it will pass. Every day we know what we need, our gut is talking to us. We know what is good for us and what makes sense. When we follow a knowing we follow what our angels want us to know. You must listen to them and ask them for help so that they know you're reaching out. You may have bought a book on self-love, but you would rather watch Netflix. We tell others who don't sense the same feeling that we are unsure of what to do. Following a feeling is not easy and others can shut us down, as they are not used to looking internally.

Protected Lesson - Step 1
Feel the feeling
Ask your gut instinct to help you, ask if this feeling is what is really going on. They say your gut instinct is never

wrong. Never ignore it, for the feeling wants you to be in tune with it. If you feel like you need guidance, say this prayer...

Lead me to the highest good, if I am lost then guide me, if I am wrong, please correct me and show me where I am supposed to go. Align me with love and follow me as I unfold on this path that you are always guiding me towards...

Say this as you feel your gut instinct kick in...

As I write this book, I know this is a hard thing to say. Sometimes we spend so much of our lives holding back our feelings, trying not to cry and trying not to react. We tell people that we're ok when deep down we are just pretending that covering up is ok when it's not. Just like how we indicate that we are going right when we drive. We should listen to that flashing light inside us that says I don't like this.

Write this prayer down, put it on a post-it, put it at your bedside or even type it in your phone, post it online and tell the universe you want to understand your feelings. This is the first step to aligning with your highest good.

Protected Lesson - Step 2
Follow through this feeling

Follow through with the commitment you make to yourself. Start listening to your body and the universe that is making that big flashlight that could light up the next chapter in your

A sound, a feather or a knowing

life. When you ask for guidance flow with it as you follow something you cannot really explain; you are listening to you and that is what's important. Following through with this feeling to me means to really go with it. If something is making me cry, now I cry not for too long but just long enough before God asks me what's that for? I am with you! The universe wants to support you, it's looking for ways that you will pick up on these tiny feelings that come up. The same way a headache can mean you need more water. It's similar. Do you have a feeling that job you are thinking of applying for might be a bad idea? Well, what if you're right? You shouldn't because you have a bigger purpose, your heart knows it and so does your gut instinct. You're right because what if... what if your body knows all the answers already?

Protected Lesson - Step 3
In the moment it might feel strange

When you follow something you're not sure about it can feel uncomfortable and scary and that's ok. Sometimes the path you didn't expect is the one to be aware of, it's about surrendering to your gut instinct and feeling and saying I am going to follow this, show me where it will lead. You will find this path connected to your gut instinct is easier than your own self sabotage.

I messaged my brother today and I told him to choose the path of least resistance. I say this because even I am still practising this as much as I can.

Protected Awakenings

There have been plenty of times in my life where I have said to the universe, I did not picture it like this, are you sure you want me to do this?

Sometimes I gulp at the realisation that I must give up my emotions and listen in to them. This may be a weird feeling you don't understand and that is ok. Change is ok and you must be open to that. Not everyone learns this simple but effective way of tuning into yourself and your body. Just by checking in with yourself you can admit that the strange feeling will not feel strange next time you will know what to do after this chapter.

Each energy centre of your body has its own biological makeup. They have their own glands, hormones, chemicals, and individual mini-brains (a plexus of neurons) and therefore their own mind. – Dr.Joe Dispenza

In Dr. Joe Dispenza's book – Becoming Supernatural he explains that each energy centre in the body has its own mini brain. One of the mini brain's is the gut instinct or as he calls it the second brain. The so called Second brain holds hundreds of millions of neurons and neural connections. When each of these mini brains are activated, they emit energy, and the action then forms in the mind.

So, understanding and being in tune with your gut instinct is key because then you can be in the moment with it before it makes up its own mind that the feeling is important or not.

A sound, a feather or a knowing

Protection that is not seen can work for you. Tell that feeling that you're glad it showed up! Follow these three steps again and again if you need to. Make a conscious effort to connect to your inner knowing and pay attention to your feelings they are there to protect you more than you will ever know.

CHAPTER 3
Your story is your story

In September 2020, I had the most horrendous nightmares while I was having lots of health issues and talking to doctors continuously and feeling like I was never getting any help. Night after night I had nightmares about different animals dying. Every night my mind would zoom in on a fox ripping open a bird or a dead hamster on the garden step and I would wake up in hot sweats questioning my whole life and what was wrong.

This energy wanted to distract me and after interrupting all the nightmares I sensed a fear building inside me.

One angel I met, my mentor and dear friend Sean G Murphy, changed my perspective on life and told me that the fox in my nightmare was eating my dreams.

I started meditating which was completely new to me. Sean, my mentor, talked about the importance of meditating, and I thought I would try in silence. I meditated for one hour and a half and I saw myself lying in bed with a golden ring all around me. I saw myself glowing and I felt like someone had

Protected Awakenings

plugged me into a phone charger to keep the light glowing as I felt weaker and weaker inside. When I looked up what this colour meant it said that if you see yellow, it represents the fear in your body.

Think about what your angel is showing you.

I would never have started meditating and seen the peace that was available to me if I had not met my mentor and good friend Sean G Murphy.

I met Sean on a zoom call. He is from Texas and from the moment I saw him speaking I was in awe of his mindset and ability to present so well while being relatable to everyone all over the world. Sean G Murphy is one of the greatest teachers I have had in my life, he is the most amazing mentor and coach. He is the Tony Robbins that everyone needs in their life! I see Sean in the same light as Tony Robbins, Sadguru, Deepak Chopra, Rhonda Byrne and many other awakened souls on Instagram who brighten my heart.

I signed up for Sean's self-talk course which was the most amazing and life changing mind shift I think I have ever been through. Not only was I changing my mindset, but I was also changing my perspective on how I viewed the world. Even though all I did was pay for a course about mental toughness, I was really being helped by an angel in my eyes because he was about to help me with the hardest chapter of my life, and I had no idea.

As I built up my meditation practice, Sean asked the whole group to meditate in silence. I remember thinking you want me, Jessica, who is always doing something, to be silent

Your story is your story

for two hours for as long as I can? Yeah right… but I thought I have to give it a go.

I lay down and thoughts rushed to me from all over the place, the more I tried to quieten my mind the more my mind wandered until I remembered once, Sean said when you have a negative thought say, **"and I love that"**. Looking back, I can see that he was saying **"get comfortable with the uncomfortable"** and you may find that it's hard until **"it's not"**. I remember hearing my parent's talking downstairs and saying, **"and I love that"**. Hearing the train speed pass by out the window I said, and **"I love that"**.

Every distraction became ok as I said, 'I love that'. Sean quotes some of the best mentors in the world and after hearing him more and more, I have felt very positive, sensing a light, and seeing things in a way I never expected to. I was surprised by how I changed my mindset and ended up speechless with more questions than I began with.

After watching an online event I tried a Kundalini meditation for protection and more alignment which my favourite teacher Gabby Bernstein has suggested. I connect to all that is good outside of me and within me. I also love a walking meditation to listen to everything I can see near and far away and pay attention to my breath as I walk.

If I didn't meditate, I would not be able to protect my energy and catch my racing mind of spiralling anxiety and and those annoying nightmares I had. There was an outside energy that was trying to tear me down. I did not want to have anything to do with the nightmares I had, and I did not want that to be my story.

Protected Awakenings

One morning I remember waking up to what wasn't a nightmare but a dream of my garden again but this time no animals. Just a white round table and a white tablecloth. I remembered this small tablecloth from when I was a child at the front of my house by the door which my mother used for the house phone. My granny came in my dream again showing me this tablecloth she made. In the vision it turned into a microscope of green embroidery that was very intricate and pretty with little green leaves. I woke up, looked up the dream searching for the word embroidery. The words jumped out at me and said… *Your story is your story,* it does not need to be fancy, you don't have to show off, leave it as it is.

I walked downstairs and asked my mum if granny had a white tablecloth with green embroidery and she said "yes, it's in the front room", she was always sewing and she made it herself. Out of nowhere I burst into tears, I knew this dream meant something and I felt a rise of emotions that I could not understand properly when the whole time my guardian angel (my grandmother Olga) was telling me that my story does not need to be sensational or dramatic, I just need to say it as it is. That is what I'm doing for you today. This is more proof of the protection that was in my dreams and in my waking life. I was crying from the power of my angel. When she was guiding me to this page immediately.

At the time I was confused, but when I thought I didn't have an amazing story. I was wrong. I was about to start a story that would help so many other people and amaze them that they wouldn't understand how I am still standing today.

Your story is your story

I think an angel can be anyone who gets you out of your negative mindset, recommends a book, helps you in your new story or frees you from something that wasn't really holding you back it just looked like it was because it's an illusion, another distraction.

The mind can be like a closed book if you close it. While your angel screams at you, you must remain open to all ideas it wants to give you.

The universe really wants you to free yourself from the lies you wake yourself up with that are not real. When you wake up to the protection all around you. You will start to see your mindset needs to change to rewrite the next page for the better.

We think that we are not able to do something new, we hold on to the old story so much that we almost always stop ourselves from what we want. Our angels watch us turning down blessings, books, friends, help, an outlet for change. Your angels have been sent to reach out to you by an invisible protection I personally call God and the angels who he puts in place to guide me, to awaken me to the truth that I am here for a reason and so are you.

Your mentor could be in a book you really want to read, a podcast you want to listen to and focus on or a motivational video. Your mentor could be someone you watch or someone who has the same core values as you. Whoever they are keep a set time and listen to them.

Your mentor can be your angel who helps you constantly and guides you to give you more energy to keep going and encourage you in the positivity you were born with as a baby.

You were not born an angry baby.—*Sean G Murphy*

While we ignore something that is there every day to help us, we are pushing away what we are praying for every night, we are just too blind to see that the key is right in front of us, right under our noses.

In my case I was praying every night that I would get help with my health issues, and I did in the end, but I was afraid to let go in the way the universe was guiding me.

Use these three steps to connect and protect your energy. Connect to the protection all around you and you will be a lot calmer and see the world in another light. Remember that your story is your story, and your path is yours don't let fear or anyone else keep you from the truth of that. Keep your eyes open for how your angel wants you to write on a fresh page to connect and write a positive story into your future.

Protected Lesson - Step 1
Meditation can help you connect to your angels

Angels cannot help you if you don't ask for help. In ***The Angel Bible by Hazel Raven*** there is so much information on every angel and what they can help you with. You can google all of them as you see the surrounding never-ending support that is available to you. Every second of your life, they are asking you to wake up, show up and keep up.

Your story is your story

Look up mediation videos, these can be as simple as three-minute sessions. When I first started guided meditations, I felt more relaxed in those three minutes than I did after an eight-hour sleep. You can have a look into what works for you and start to see how you can improve your concentration and your way of connecting to your inner peace.

As you mediate learn to become quiet in your body and then your mind and be aware of the support that is beneath you, holding you up. This is one energy. Above you whether that is God, the universe or whoever you believe in, let this spirit guide you not just in your meditation but also throughout your day. As you begin to practice you will get use to this way of calm and newfound peace. In this book I will mention God, I will speak of the universe but most importantly I want you to hear me out. I believe in the goodness of the world that you saw with the eyes of a child. If you want to use the word Universe more than God, I'm ok with that and if you are not sure about either and you just want to learn more that is ok too. If you have a relationship with God then I hope you connect to my words and prayers and additional methods that I have learned over time and just have a go.

If you mediate for one minute today that is a start and if you pray and sit in silence with God for one minute you may have the most peace you ever had and might feel suddenly overwhelmed with a relaxed feeling in that present moment.

Meditation is not just sitting there cross legged. For me it's about relaxing into the knowing that what I'm doing is grounding myself into, my natural state and my heart that

Protected Awakenings

wants to be calm, wants to connect and wants to be able to sit in that place of great energy that God gave me. To serve others and to live in my light that the angels showed me. I am more comfortable lying down flat when I meditate. I only started sitting up when I meditate a few months ago.

I grew up thinking that spirituality and religion were very separate, however I learnt that this is not true. I learnt that Oprah has meditations on God and searching and connecting to light is different from the stereotypical fortune teller mediums who practise telling people the future. I personally prefer to connect to God, however after taking a trip into depression and uncertainty, I continued to believe in the Universe which brought me back to God. God continued to talk to me while I journaled and meditated. I have realised that I have always been a spiritual person since I was a child. What if I was always meditating?... just not in the concentrated way I do nowadays.

When you meditate you might feel sleepy and that's ok, that means you need to sleep away all the anxiety that you have been holding on to every day that will stop, let it leave your body. When I first started meditating, I would yawn and have the best naps in the middle of the day. When everyone else was panicking about covid I was asleep and then researching and reading more about spirituality and connecting to source.

Meditation can also be pure concentration, anything where you feel a constant energy you can tune into it and start to think about where you feel at peace and fulfilled at the same time.

Your story is your story

For example, I love to swim, when I swim, I like to glide to the bottom of the pool and rub my tummy on the pool floor holding my breath for a long time, listening to complete silence and subtle splashes of other people's feet around me. That was the intense focus that I gave myself in that moment. Ask yourself when you have this focus. Is it when running? Or cooking? What helps you to zone out and tune in with yourself while you're enjoying the present moment so much you zoom in and everything else takes a sidestep as though time stopped for you to move your energy into a better place, I call peace.

My brother José is a DJ *@treehouse43* and when he describes the structure of his mixes, I realised that this is his meditation. When he focuses on the next song coming in and the excitement of not knowing where his mix will take him. I saw and told him it's his meditation. Some of us always meditate. We go for that thing that we feel we excel at and we get a rush from, because we are in this flow and nothing compares to this feeling once we understand it.

Once you have learnt this step you can connect to your angels in your meditation. Ask them to lead you to where your heart should go.

Ask your angels to heal you and tell them what's worrying you, give it over. The Universe does not like (I need) worrying energy. It's not yours anymore. Focus on the angels that want to cover you and complete you with the light that will fill your whole body.

Say this prayer...

Protected Awakenings

Write it down with me in your journal, say it in your mind or get quiet and focus.

I (your *name*) want to be more aware of you today...

Show me my real story

Angels/ spirit/ universe/God/who I believe in...

I give my needy energy to you, take away (_the situation_) and I want to rewrite my story, so it is mine and mine only. For my story is my story and you know the ending that is for the highest good. Guide me, love me and show me what I need to see. For you know the angel I need to see, what's best for me and what should really happen for me to stay true to me.

I hope you will feel better after this prayer, repeat it every day after every challenge you face when you don't know what direction to go in.

A Post-it on the fridge, writing on a bookmark or writing all over this book would make me so happy. Writing yes, I pray this prayer can be your first step to a new start.

Protected Lesson - Step 2
Get a mentor! Feed your mind with light and resilience...

Not all mentors are people I have met or people I know personally. I have not yet met Sean, but I am so grateful I can call him to change my perspective and make me see that the tunnel has lots of light at the end of it. Even though there was

Your story is your story

an outside energy working hard to distract me I have lots of tools now to capture love, light and change my viewpoint in my heart.

I have watched another mentor rewire her brain by going live on social media saying an affirmation and then picking up a skipping rope and skipping to get the affirmation into her body. We all need a wake-up call to shake off energy we don't like and get back into the light we need.

Your mentor could be a book you really want to focus on, maybe it's a podcast that speaks to you, the motivation you need to face the day. Listen to it every day, make it a habit and see the light in them. When a mentor suggests something, that you are not use to or something new, be open to it and be ready to see things in a new way.

Protected Lesson - Step 3
Write on a fresh page

While you journey into this new story, you should also journal your thoughts on the outside. View yourself as the third person in the room. Be aware of your positive thoughts, your negative thoughts, and all the ways in which those words then leak into your mind, actions, and your words.

Take notice of how you could possibly be pushing your stubborn heart away from what could go on the fresh page.

Sit in your heart when you write, write to the angels, ask them to take something away. (Think about what this means for you)

Protected Awakenings

Ask them to heal you, ask God, your angels / spirit guides / whoever you believe in to rewrite your story and write the real story in your heart.

Be honest, if you're not happy, say this prayer:

Please channel my writing and help me start a fresh day, a fresh page of my story of love, light, and pure energy so that I can become clearer about the future I want to connect to with your support this time...

Meditate and find the mentor who will guide you to be what your guardian angel wants you to be. Invest in yourself, that could mean downloading a new meditation app and starting a new focus. It could be a book. Trust yourself that you will be happy and free. Start to connect to angels in your meditation and choose how to connect to the prayer I gave you. Ask and then write it down, say it in your mind. Focus on it repeatedly when you feel you need it. Rewrite your story of how protected you are, and what it means to you to feel more held in the truth of your heart. Journal your experiences and see yourself as the other person in the room, write that letter to your future self and into this new adventure. Let go of fear-based stories and tell yourself every day that your angels surround you and that you are never alone. Your heart is always being listened to every second of the day.

Journal through your new story and God/the universe will support your every step. Keep writing as you will not only see the connections as you go but more so when you look back, you will see why your writing supports you as you

Your story is your story

ask more questions and note of how you want your story to be for your future.

I understand the steps above can be steps out of your comfort zone and that is ok. Take it slowly, meditating for five minutes can change your day completely. Journaling for five minutes, writing down a prayer for five minutes can change your mindset. Have a go and see how you feel.

In the next chapter I will show you how I journaled about an earth angel, and let God/ the Universe hold my hand through the most challenging part of my story, however I found more support than ever and I want you to see this in your life.

CHAPTER 4
Let the universe hold your hand

On the 21st of September 2020 I called Ronda Bird Parker but before I tell you about our phone call, I will tell you how we met.

I wrote in my journal about Ronda from East Texas, who helped me more than she will ever know. When I first went on Sean's calls, Ronda would start his daily mentoring call with a prayer, or she would end the call and wrap it up with her conclusion of how she heard the message given that day. Every time she spoke, I felt so drawn to her, like a moth flying towards the light. After a while there was a whole community of us that became close friends, but I knew there was something about Ronda that I just couldn't put my finger on.

The more I watched her energy, her essence, and her light I was in awe of her, and I didn't even know her whole story.

I remembered telling Ronda about a film I watched and how I couldn't forget it. Ronda told me to be careful with

Protected Awakenings

what I watch and the negative impact it could have and play on my mind. I mentioned my back pain and how much it had been bothering me and she said I should give it to God.

I had the worst back pain and getting up every day ignoring it and being the strong girl, I thought I was. I called the doctor about my back, she said If I ever can't feel anything from the waist down then I must call A+E immediately, but she said this won't happen and it's the worst-case scenario and she prescribed some pain killers.

When I explained where the pain was to Ronda, she said all you need to do is say *"God, hold my hand"* and with a smile I suddenly felt instantly sleepy, a sense of peace filled my whole body.

I didn't quite know what to say so I listened, my relationship with God was not as strong as it was when I was a teenager, so it felt strange to even think of handing the pain over. I surrendered into what she said. As soon as I took on what Ronda said even though I didn't want to accept it, I felt this whole wave of calm, flow over my whole body.

I told her and she said, "Then sleep Jessica." I don't even remember hanging up or switching off my phone. Leaving it on my desk, I fell asleep, and the pain dulled.

As soon as I came off facetime with Ronda, I had fallen asleep for the first time in two days.

From that moment the real work had begun. I had been helped by a real-life earth angel and to this day I don't think I would be here typing up this book without her.

Let the universe hold your hand

A few days later the 30th of September 2020, I fainted on the bathroom floor and I couldn't get up again. The worst-case scenario the doctor talked about had happened before I could blink. I overheard my brother talking to my mum on the phone and I asked my dad to bring me another ice pack for my back because the pain was unbearable. I prayed. I prayed to God saying, Lord, whatever this pain is take it away from me. I was in agony and my muscles spasmed so much I couldn't get up off the floor. The pain was excruciating and stopped me from doing anything.

Ronda messaged me straight away saying God brought my face to her. I was completely shocked. I prayed and Ronda was there in a flash, I only realise this from reading my journal. I told her what was happening, and she said she felt like she was not helping, I thanked her and said no you have helped me so much.

Exactly what the doctor said wouldn't happen, happened. I felt nothing from the waist down and I had wet myself, but I didn't feel it happen. I had zero feeling from my waist down.

Lying there helplessly I remembered a quote I had seen by Gabby Bernstein that said "not all storms come to disrupt your life, some storms come to clear the path."

I remembered this and I told my parents I had to go to hospital while I lay on my bedroom floor; too scared to tell them that I could not feel anything from my waist down.

I knew something was wrong and it was dangerous whatever It was. I knew God would hold my hand and I had to face something not seeing that the storm was stirring inside of me.

Protected Awakenings

What my parents didn't know was that I was being protected, surrounded, and loved through a horrendous experience.

From that day forward and still to this day I surrendered. I completely came back to God. I handed everything over and said **"God hold my hand"**. We can do this anytime and with anything in our lives that we are struggling with.

When you surrender, your ego gets really annoyed it says to you that you should not give up the pain and struggle that you spent so long holding on to.

The moment I said hands up, I can't take this, I surrender, everything changed.

When we don't surrender, we hold onto expectation, and we think we can do it on our own. When we do this, we push away God, The Universe and all the angels. We are telling them that we don't need them, and we don't want our prayers answered. When the paramedics arrived at my house, I couldn't get off the floor. I said at one point that's it, I can't do it, I will have to stay here. The pain completely catapulted me into screaming and crying. I cannot describe the unbearable pain I had to bear to stand up.

My mentor, Sean, says your ego stands for Edging God Out. I think the more we rely on our own strength we tell our ego that it's going to be ok, but it's never good enough for our ego.

We tell the Universe that we can cope with the struggle so then the Universe dishes out more struggle to match with

Let the universe hold your hand

the frequency we are vibrating at which is pain, suffering and struggle.

You cannot accept protection if you just keep putting bodyguards in front of your house that are not talking to you. The moment you say I don't know what direction to go in, but I know I need help, help me know which way to go. You will feel relief instantly.

When relief comes, accept it, open your heart to it. The Universe wants to protect you and hold you. The Universe does not want to see you in pain, struggling and hating life. The Universe wants to love you, light you up inside to see you living your best life.

To do this I will show you some prayers and ways of surrendering that may guide you in the right direction.

Protected Lesson - Step 1
Write a surrender letter

Then it hit me, when I was crying for help on the floor when I couldn't get up, God really called Ronda to speak to me immediately.

When I look back at my journal, I can see that I prayed the prayer Ronda told me to pray. When I said **God hold my hand,** that's exactly what he did. I was on the floor crying and she was there messaging me straight away, "maybe I can help you to ask for help to surrender and reach out too."

Protected Awakenings

Write to God/Universe/Angel or even your deceased family member who has always loved you and listened to you

You can write this prayer, say it in your mind or out loud.

I (_____your name_____)

God/Universe/Angels

Please hear my prayer

Please act and send the best resolution for me now. (WHO YOU BELIEVE IN) Hold my hand, for you know what's best for me and my life. You see the bigger picture and I will accept whatever is for the highest good.

I surrender to you, and I open my heart to you all as you hold me in your love and light.

Thank you, angels, for holding me as I surrender this situation to you_____fill in the blank.

For I know you hear my name and cover me in the protection you have always promised.

To you I pray.

Protected Lesson - Step 2
Allow the universe to hold you while angels find you

Once you surrender, make sure it's with everything. You can't thank your angels and say but I have a headache. It's

Let the universe hold your hand

like saying I trust you with one suitcase and not the other. Give the angels your whole life even the things you don't tell anyone. A woman once told me you can't believe in God and not trust him, or say you read the bible sometimes, but life is not that great right now. Your angels are holding you even when they are completely invisible.

Letting the Universe hold you is an everyday practice. When I am at my lowest, which happens now and again, if I slip up on my spiritual practices like my meditations, prayers or reading my devotional **(Jesus Calling – by Sarah Young)**. If I fall down the rabbit hole with Alice in Wonderland, I am carrying an anxiety that is not mine. I hand it over and my energy changes in an instant. Some call this the Holy Spirit, Gabby Bernstein calls it the holy instant.

Tell the universe thank you for holding on to me and for this awareness and this place. Thank you for holding me as I take the next step. The relief is yours, breathe out and hand over everything.

Smile… you don't own all the problems in the world.
—Unknown

Have faith in knowing you are being held, and letting go, knowing the situation has been given over to a higher power. I also surrender my life goals, my manifestations, visualisations and plans to God/Universe daily because he knows more than me and I hope this book will awaken YOU. For he knows what you personally need to be awakened to. I will admit it is hard letting go because we are so used to holding on trying to keep it all together and not letting anyone see through the mask, we put up to pretend that everything is ok when it's not.

The Japanese say we have three faces:

The first face, you show the world.

The second face, you show to your close friends, and your family.

The third face, you never show anyone. It is the truest reflection of who you are. – Unknown

That third face, the one that you see in the mirror and sigh…. give that face to the higher power whom you connect with.

Say this prayer...

Thank you God/Universe/Angels

For holding me in this space, giving me the angels. I will let you come to me, hold my hand, and thank you that I hear you, see you and feel your wisdom light up within me. I want to know you and trust that I will follow the right path you guide me to every day.

Write anything you wish here or in a journal, scribble, don't think, just write, and let support come to you and through you.

_____

_____

_____

Let the universe hold your hand

Protected Lesson - Step 3
Be Open and Fill up with Faith

Fill up with faith that everything will be ok in the end. As I look back on my life, even though I am only 30 years old, I feel like an old soul. With all I have been through, and I wouldn't put it all in here because I really believe a higher power does not want me to, I have been ok, why?

I now realise I had protection all around me that you could be opened up to at any time. I want to give you the space to unload that suitcase of struggle. No one asked you to carry around what's weighing you down.

Filling up with faith is something you can do anytime in your life. I never appreciated how powerful prayer can be until more and more people around the world prayed for me and I felt better almost instantly. I swear it is stronger than when you watch a superhero heal in a film. The same way we refill a glass of water, fill yourself up with love, faith, thankfulness that everything in your life is taken care of by a higher power. Imagine that higher power is holding the glass of water that is your life, this is all taken care of before you do anything.

Faith is the invisible whisper that says I know there is something better than this. I have heard others say that they have crazy faith, that everything will be ok. Crazy faith that someone else (The man upstairs) is watching you with every event in your life and holding you up while you cope with today.

Protected Awakenings

Say this Prayer:

God   /Universe/Angels

To who I connect with...

I open up now and I want you to fill me with love and light, please lead me into faith in you. I always open and trust with my full trust in you, I thank you that my life ahead of me is taken care of now that you really hear me with my hands open. You knew me before I was born, and you see me now with the path that you want for me and my life, for I know there is always hope and even more blessings in you.

Write this down today, sit with it, think about it, read it tomorrow before work, email this to yourself... Prayer is practice, talking to a higher power is practice, and believing in general is a practice and practising to be confident that someone else is listening, is how you start to really connect and see that your prayer will come true.

Accept that a higher power wants to help you. When you open your heart to the light, only then can the light take all the darkness, sadness, pain, grief, depression, confusion, anxiety and fear that is not yours.

The Universe will never let the darkness win and it has no right to be in you. You were not born an angry baby, remember any kind of pain, depression or anxiety were never in you and don't believe that you just got depressed, it's a lie, hand it over now, a higher power held you and said you are meant to be here, and I want you to have an abundance of

Let the universe hold your hand

blessings that is your true heart and to live in the truth that you are meant to be your true happy self by connecting to your heart.

Opening your heart takes practice and sometimes it's a space that people forget about because we spend so much time overthinking all day.

Breathe in and take notice of your heart. Notice your breath and breathe in deeply.

Breathe in and count to four

Breathe out for four

Then say this prayer *God/Universe/Angels...*
I open up to you now.

As soon as you do this you are acknowledging the heart that God/Universe gave you and the heart that wants to be itself in peace and light.

A heart that wants love, feels love and looks for love and follows love.

God/Universe is the same, it wants to love you, support you and hold you with an invisible protection that is always available to you wherever you are. As you read this you are being held. Feel the floor, your feet grounded and the space you're in is your energy and your energy is more powerful than anything else on the planet. We are energy, we see energy, we add to the positivity or negativity all around us every moment of our lives.

Protected Awakenings

Each of us is attracting in every moment of our lives. So, when you feel that the law isn't working for you because you don't have what you want, realise that the law is responding to you. You are either attracting what you want, or you are attracting the absence of what you want. The law is still working.
– Rhonda Byrne

Do this practice every day and you are telling your heart it is held in a safe space. When your heart connects to your breath you will feel it hold you. Open your heart and let the light in again.

This practice can be done once a day, before you go to bed or when you wake up. Do this as much as you can, and you will see a difference in the way you feel.

To let the God/The Universe, hold your hand, use these steps and surrender. This is crucial and something I still practise myself everyday. Sometimes I feel it's all I do. Give over what's worrying you. If there is something keeping you up at night, or something consuming your life and you feel you can't let it go, let your guides hold you, pray and let go. Fill yourself up with faith and do this daily and know in your heart and mind that you will always be taken care of this is the truest form of protection to me and I hope you learn this beautiful lesson for yourself. I know some of my chapters will be a discovery and a new way of thinking but take from this what you need and interpret how you see the world.

I want this book to be yours to cross out a word, to rip out a page and use a prayer next time you face difficulty

Let the universe hold your hand

because this book is yours and God wants your heart to know that the rib cage around your heart is protecting your world that is yours. In the next chapter I will share with you how I have been awakened to a whole world of angels that actually support us all and guide us so that we can protect our family, friends and all those who are screaming for someone to save them. The Universe uses us to help save a life when we thought we just went out to grab lunch.

I want to show you how several angels fill the world and make the world spin around to help everyone and protect those who need protection the most.

CHAPTER 5
Several angels fill our world

In January 2022, I was sitting in a coffee shop typing up what I thought would be my last chapters of this book and I noticed the energy shift in the room. I looked up at a woman about to sit down next to me and she placed a book on the table. She got up to get her coffee and I looked over, but I couldn't see the book clearly. When she came back, I smiled at her and asked, "What are you reading? "She smiled back and showed me a book of affirmations called *'You are amazing! By Debbi Marco'*.

I told her I was reading something similar that someone suggested I should read. Her infectious smile started to make me more curious about her. She introduced herself and said her name is Jolanta, we clicked like we had known each other forever and we couldn't stop talking. We got on the subject of spirituality, which is what I love to talk about, I was so excited.

Protected Awakenings

I told her about my book and how my health issues and overcoming them inspired me to write. Explaining my story I said that some people are living for the second time. Jolanta told me her story. She completely drew me in. She said years ago she was in a car accident, and she saw her whole life flash before her eyes like a movie. At this point I straightaway thought of my friend Eugenia who was also in a car accident and who has had many awakenings, but she couldn't really explain hers which I felt I really related to.

I tend to sense things before they happen, and I feel I was thinking about my friend Eugenia even before Jolanta mentioned her accident. Feeling like this story was going to get worse my gut instinct got quiet, and I wasn't ready for the story I'm about to tell you or the stories I'm obsessed with which made me want to write this book and prove that we do live for a second time.

My brain works so fast Eugenia kept flashing in my mind I was wondering if she was ok in this present moment and why I felt so connected to her. Focusing more on Jolanta she said Jesus held her hands and said, **"you must go back to earth; you can't go up there"**. At that point I knew my book would be even more special and she was there to tell me that I had a bigger purpose in my life, that I now HAD to publish this book to help others have any kind of awakening as close as this one. Jolanta explained it all so well and talked of a bright white light and I was completely captured and wide eyed about what I was hearing, feeling closer to God.

Jolanta is a spiritual healer and so calm and her energy radiates so close you feel like you're in a fluffy blanket and

Several angels fill our world

this was the first time I had met her. She said that she believes that God's people really do gravitate towards each other and that's why we got on so well and connected. After hearing that story, it was more proof to me that awakenings are real, they protect us, and we must awaken to the truth that there is a higher power and that there is more than this short materialistic illusion of life that some of us don't understand. For there is always a presence, pushing us, leading us to more and protecting us, to stick together, enlighten one another and listen to an inner peace we feel within us that we're all born with.

My dad is from Venezuela which is actually what inspired this book cover, my father and my brother Jose' have been to the Angel falls the waterfall at the front of this book which is where I always wanted to go since I was a little girl. When my uncle Thomas called my father and heard I wasn't well they said I should meditate and pray to Archangels Raphael and Michael who are healing angels. What my uncle didn't know was that I had already started meditations for healing.

If I told you now about all the angels there are in the world I would run out of space, there are so many. I used to read about fairies and angels, and I thought they sounded like the best make-believe creatures I had ever heard about. I always wanted to write a book about fantasy or science fiction. I was never interested in writing about nonfiction, but here we are.

I know I am being brave telling you what I believe in and how someone saved my life. I believe that earth angels

Protected Awakenings

walk amongst us, I believe that I have met more angels along with my granny and Ronda and the friend I made in my last year of high school who understood me while I was bullied by everyone else. Another friend I met was Holly Livingstone who shares my belief in angels and has a connection to her guardian angel. When I was doing a lifeguarding course before I went to teach swimming abroad, we became great friends. God works in mysterious ways and most of the time in a way you never imagined.

We have healing angels, vets who have the gift of helping animals. There are people who help those humans in suffering and in pain, nurses, doctors who think they are just doing their job, but they are saving lives every day. There are creative angels, I learned this is my way of helping the world, whether it's dancing, writing for you now or painting, there are songwriters and poets who write about angels and near-death experiences that surprise us all. If singers and actors are angels then they show us another viewpoint of the world, what if I told you all these angels, I have described are being used by God to be a domino effect on us all.

Everyone is assigned an angel the moment they are born. From one person that sings that song that was played at someone's funeral comforted by an angel's voice or someone who speaks to a doctor who is just explaining facts, it's all help from the universe this is how we manage to cope and survive in these testing times. God/Universe/ Angels are always working to embrace us, but we are too blind to see it.

Several angels fill our world

We live in a big universe which is made up of lightworkers all around us. Meanwhile others have no idea they are an angel to you and me.

I am so thankful for every angel that has ever been in my presence that it gives me goosebumps and strength just thinking about it now. I have had many amazing people in my life who have redirected me to the light.

Now I see the earth angels and how they help the world and how life is happening for us and not to us.

Use these three steps to connect to an angel and ask for guidance in your life.

Protected Lesson - Step 1
Pray to connect to the universe all around you

"As below, so above; and as above so below. With this knowledge alone you may work miracles."

The Emerald Tablet (Circa 5,000 – 3,000 BC)

Write this in a journal, say it out loud or in your mind.

Lord, Angel of God, my guardian angel to you I pray, lead me, guide me, hear me, I know you will never leave my side ever and never today. Awaken my heart every time and any time you say it is needed for I want to be changed and consumed by your loving presence so warm and full of light.

When you ask for clear directions, you may not always see it right away. It could be in two-days' time, but when you

Protected Awakenings

say such powerful prayers, you are opening up to someone who has loved you all your life and watches you complain. We walk through life complaining about every little thing that happens to us thinking no one cares and this is not true, but what would you do if you met God/Universe/Angels and they showed you what your life could have looked like if you had been connected to your maker 24/7 and living in a constant flow of love?

Protected Lesson - Step 2
Ask for the right angel you need

Write here if you want, say this out loud or in your mind.

God/Universe/Angels please send the angel now that you know I need first. Let my eyes see the presence that you have sent me in any sign that comes to me so naturally. Send me an earth angel and turn my heart to understand this power and presence

_____

_____

_____

Look up the angels, I like to call Archangel Raphael for healing and Archangel Michael and Gabriel who are mentioned in the Old Testament and in times of need, but we must tell them we need help. They can't help if we are not open.

Several angels fill our world

Protected Lesson - Step 3
Invite the angels into your life

Angels excite me, leave me filled with more love to fill others. People talk about them and throw the word angel around like it's not real. Calling a child an angel or just using it as a saying. We have artwork of angels all around the world. We have millions of songs, stories and inspiration about angels. Just type angel or angels into a search engine and you will realise that people are serious about them and have seen them in dreams in real life, in signs and prayed to them for years.

Angels bring God's warming love and capture us with a huggable light that we are so drawn too.

Other angels are there to comfort us or bring God back in our lives like Ronda Bird Parker did for me.

Some believe more angels are amongst us to be here before the end days.

To be open to all I have told you

Say this prayer

God/Universe, guide your angels/spirits that hear my prayer, sit with me as I call your name, guide me and assist me with all areas of my life I find challenging as you light the path and the answer for me.

Use these prayers as and when you need them, connect to the one YOUR heart opens up to because this book is about your heart. It's about your story and the

Protected Awakenings

higher power that is drawing you and calling you while you unfold these pages in front of this universe I am so proud of you for just witnessing this moment right now. Reading these prayers that are channelled through me so YOU can fill up with faith that you are being heard, protected now and always. Circle or highlight your favourite prayer and repeat it and claim it, it's now yours…

I was going to put this at the end of this book, but this story is so powerful, and I want to really show you not just my story but the stories that others have shared with me and awakened me to that I am not alone in what I believe. Some have awakenings all day and constantly write them down some have awakenings in dreams like I did in chapter one and others speak of seeing a white light after a near-death experience and I am absolutely intrigued when I hear them and that is why I wanted to write this, because no one is talking about this, no one is looking at the good we have in the world that I call Jesus and God and others call mother nature is holding us here for a bigger reason.

Now buckle up because in the next chapter I'm going to be very honest and share with you a time I thought I wouldn't come back from, but God needed me to awaken and awaken quickly.

I will talk about storms and how to face them. For you may have had storms in your life and you have never been able to face them, but I will walk you through it so next time you can be held during that time.

CHAPTER 6
The Storm

The whole of 2019 changed my life, and it was the start of covid spreading but people were not told, it was kept hush hush in some parts of the world in early November people were getting sick and they didn't know why, one of my friends said he was in Thailand and was told by a tour guide to wear a mask but they didn't explain why, just that he had to wear it. I was arguing with my boyfriend at the time constantly. I wanted to move out into a flat with him, but we couldn't find anywhere to live and the rent in London is so expensive. We were both very creative, very stubborn at heart even though we loved each other so hard we would have done anything to make one another happy.

 I was travelling on the train every weekend for an hour and a half just to see his handsome face and be able to just have a hug from the one person who understood me inside out. All my friends were in awe of how in love we were. We planned holidays, went to Majorca and found out that the day we flew back was the day that Majorca had an awful storm that took over and lots of people died. If we stayed

Protected Awakenings

one more day, we would have been caught up in it but again we were protected thanks to God. All my life, I have said "well that was close" thinking about how lucky I was to not get caught up in the storm and flooding that was all over the news. I decided to fly to Kos that year to teach swimming in April which my boyfriend of several years was not happy about. I just wanted an escape from the anxiety I had felt that my life wasn't moving forward, and it suffocated me.

Flying to Kos felt like a big mistake after a six-year-old boy walked out of a hotel room while his parents were asleep and drowned in a swimming pool early one morning and then someone called for help. Six of us did CPR I watched a man do compressions too fast and I started counting and took over. I got water out of the dead body, and it took me a long time to get over the post-traumatic stress I had from the most traumatic scene of my life. It literally looked like the end of the world, people screaming and running around. After I had spent a year in London having random panic attacks even while I was teaching, on the train, in nightclubs, I was losing myself.

I was the calm one in that situation, like an awakening I watched everything in slow motion and acted like I was going to bring this boy back to life. After talking to many people, they all said God knows how long the boy had been under water before someone pulled him out and the facts helped me give it to God. Over and over and still to this day I was completely broken, even seeing the story was on the internet, and in the newspapers made me sick to my stomach.

The Storm

That day I cycled back to my gorgeous apartment, I swerved straight into a car, crashed and dislocated my knee, only for my manager to tell me the news that the boy didn't come back. I wrapped and tied up my knee with the wet swim shorts in my bag and hobbled to the nearest hotel with my push bike. I walked in crying asking for a taxi and the sweetest woman drove me back to my apartment down the road. That's when I surrendered physically.

I called my mum and cried, called my boyfriend and cried to the love of my life who took me to therapy, watched my random unexplained panic attacks for a year. I told him what happened and it was as though he couldn't take anymore so we broke up.

I was in pieces, mentally, physically and emotionally.

I had physio and took a while before I could walk again. I had spent six months working in Ibiza which I manifested and prayed for and another six months in Tenerife which I absolutely loved but going to Kos really broke me. My confidence dropped and I didn't know what was next. I flew back and lived with my parents. I got calls from my ex, but I kept telling him I dislocated my knee, and I couldn't walk, I was just pushing him away more and more because I was so deeply hurt and felt abandoned after being so far away from him.

In November 2019, I applied for a Swim Manager job at the swimming pool where I had learnt to swim when I was Little. My mum says she wanted me to swim because I had asthma and the doctor said it would be good for

Protected Awakenings

me, I loved swimming and was always passionate about it. I was approaching 29 and I thought I need the money and I'm getting older. I had a few friends at work who encouraged me to apply for the job but looking back my heart wasn't really in it; pressing send on the email made me sick to my stomach. My gut instinct was screaming No don't do it. So I ignored my gut instinct and I worked too much.

I worked full time and did everything for everyone but myself. I literally lost myself in the job because I lost the love of my life of five years. I kept the wedding dress in my favourites folder on my phone and I didn't have a life. I just wanted to work and throw myself into something else and pray that it worked out.

I had flashbacks in the middle of the night of the little boy in Kos, dead at the side of the pool, but this time I didn't have therapy for it. Thankfully the flashbacks started fading away after a few months. I was getting slower and slower and had many appointments with doctors who said they wanted me to come in for yet another blood test after doing ten already and they said they didn't know what was wrong with me, but they needed a specialist. I cried, I knew something was up, but I didn't know what it was. One day I told a friend at work I think it's cancer as I was feeling weaker and weaker.

Straightaway she said, "no don't you dare say that it's not, you'll be fine". My gut instinct did not agree, and I carried on working. I was selling swimming lessons and covering for teachers, feeling so faint. I don't know how

The Storm

I was so strong. I think I was just very disciplined and the good girl in me said you must keep working hard, when you work hard everything will come to you. In my mind I thought that once I had the important job, I'd have the house and after the house I might have a life. God must have laughed so hard at me and my plans. Everyone at work could see I was getting weaker and weaker. I always had a cold or was recovering from one and I could feel my immune system was very low. I always had back pain, was constantly tired, couldn't concentrate, had post-it-notes for everything. I wanted to sleep constantly, and I was happy I didn't faint when I got home.

The manager called me in and said I failed my probation, but God was really protecting me from covid and the job that could have killed me. I went home crying my eyes out, not knowing that the world was about to go into lockdown and how everyone's lives were at a standstill and the world would face its own storm called Covid-19. I lost my job; I broke up with my new boyfriend of about three months just before, he admitted that he had kissed his manager at a party. I got up out of his bed, got dressed and went home. I never reacted because I had promised myself that I would not shout, argue or give myself anymore stress.

I wanted peace in my heart and in my life. My health only made me feel even worse. Christmas 2019 I didn't go to my work Christmas party because I was on my period for four months losing about two pints of blood a day. I was losing weight and I felt like I wanted to throw up daily. My father caught covid and he had the worst asthma attacks, so

Protected Awakenings

we were shouting at doctors to get the right medication for him, and we had to nurse him back to health while he was slowing down.

He couldn't breathe and started to get brain fog so bad he could not even string a sentence together. As everyone was struggling with covid, my family acted like a mini pharmacy looking after our immune systems and luckily, we got through it all, but I still had no idea what was wrong with me.

The morning before I ended up in hospital, I remembered this quote.

"Not all storms come to disrupt your life, some storms come to clear the path."—Gabby Bernstein

I kept trying to work out what it meant to me and why it was still ringing in my head. A few months before this, I had been reading Gabby Bernstein's books about spirituality and learning new things and seeing spirituality from a different perspective. Reading her book 'Super Attractor', it was like I was reading about God in a spiritual way, and I was so curious about the book. Many parts of this book made my heart expand and I tried to believe that there was peace out there, even though I thought 'maybe not for me'.

There were massive dark clouds in the sky, and I was staring into space knowing deep down it meant something. I knew my gut feeling said this is bad and whatever it was, it was in the air, and it frightened me so much.

The Storm

I went on Instagram and there it was staring at me, the quote about the storm again, but this time it changed me. This time I read it like some storms don't come and break your life some storms come to make it better and that this was leading me in another direction. But I knew the actual storm was going to change me more than the year I just had.

In the middle of the pandemic, when people were so afraid of covid and hospitals, I wanted to send myself into the fire pit.

A few days before that my mum's friend Angie and someone who is now my dearest friend also, sent me a video of a motivational speaker, I don't remember his name, but he talked about driving through the storm. A girl was driving in heavy rain, she could hardly see the cars in front of her. She said to her father that she couldn't drive in the rain as it was too heavy and dangerous. He told her to keep driving. Although she was so scared she carried on and saw other cars stopping because it was so intense. The windscreen wipers were moving so fast, but they weren't helping. The girl turned to her father and said she couldn't see anything and couldn't do it, but he told her to keep going.

I remember someone saying if you're going through hell, keep going, why would you want to stop in hell?... Go through and believe you will make it out. That came to mind as I watched this video, constantly thinking that everything I watch and read is a sign and it means something. I was being a detective trying to work it out.

Protected Awakenings

So back to this video I watched, and I was in awe of the gruelling determination that her father had to make sure his daughter kept going through. I feel as though my father has always done this with me, reminding me how resilient I am and how confident I am to be able to get through anything as he has always worked hard himself for our family. As the weather calmed down and the rain got lighter and the clouds cleared, the father told his daughter to look behind her and tell him what she saw. The girl looked in the rear-view mirror and said there's no one. The father said, "that's right, there is no one there because they are all still stuck in the storm, too scared to go through it".

With this video in my mind, I really believe it was meant to be and God wanted me to see in a visual way what I needed, this was another awakening. I know at this point you have seen all my devastating awakenings; I have had so many that I have lost count. It was as if God was preparing me for what was about to come, I really felt that.

I had asked for help all year and now my body was breaking and screaming, and the pain was indescribable. I was rushed to the hospital by Ambulance.

After multiple tests, going from ward to ward, fainting on nurses, being put back in bed half conscious and taking lots of tablets not even knowing where I was, a woman called Vana, and a doctor called Elvis came into the room. Vana had green eyes and her soul was pure and I felt like I had seen her before, I felt like I knew her already. With her mask on, she held my hand and spoke to me gently. She spoke very slowly, at this point I was heavily drugged up on painkillers,

The Storm

antibiotics and lots of tablets that I struggled to remember what they were all for. She said, "We have done some tests and you have cancer". My first thought was omg it makes so much sense. I didn't think the worst, I honestly thought now I will get help. My soul knew, my heart knew, and I had waited a year to find out.

I went to the doctors so much and I asked so many questions and I never got an answer for what my gut instinct kept tuning into, I wanted to know what was wrong. I wanted someone, anyone to tell me why. I asked God pushing myself into more anxiety worrying about not getting help but this time I finally got an answer. I wasn't tired or depressed, I wasn't a failure or losing myself, I really was sick, like my gut instinct tried to tell me and I ignored it over and over until my body broke. What I didn't realise was I saved my own life along with God's help, and a whole collection of angels who I will celebrate here, and this is how my real story came out of me.

I didn't want to tell you all this. Even now my ego says that I failed, and I shouldn't share everything that changed me, but this is the most vulnerable part of my heart and so much happened when I lived my life without God. I lost it all, but he saved me in the process.

God, Ronda Bird-Parker, Sean G Murphy and Danijela Jukic along with calling my family every second kept my mindset together while I was drifting around in hospital.

One morning in the worst hospital I could have gone to, a nurse asked me if I was able to stand up for an X-ray.

Protected Awakenings

Without even letting me think about it, she walked out of the room and had organised for someone to take me there. I was in so much pain and my back felt awful. I went to the X-ray room on a bed they transferred me onto, I was shattered from just moving sideways and rolling. As I could barely sit up, I looked at the nurse and said I feel faint. Which were the same words I said every time I tried to get up. The nurse looked at me and said no, "you'll be alright". I fainted and fell to the floor for the third time in what felt like 3 days. As I slowly came round, I cried in pain. I thought, God, why am I getting no help, I am in hospital? I thought this doesn't make sense.

As I gained consciousness again, I could feel my bones weaken and shake every muscle spasm out of control again. The nurses tried to help me up, but I wouldn't let them as my back would not cooperate with me. The pain was taking over, and I knew I could only use my muscles on my left side because there was no pain there. At that point I was screaming and shouting in agony. I felt sorry for everyone in that room, my inner child was now screaming and crying, it all came out. I could only get up a certain way because that was how I got up in my house, when the paramedics came and every other time, I was helpless on the floor. One nurse put his foot out so he was in my way, and I couldn't move because they were scared, I would hit my head and faint again. He was stopping me from moving the way I wanted. I was half naked begging them to let me get back on the bed to lie down.

The Storm

Two people walked outside and discussed putting me in a hoist to get me back on the bed. My mother overheard them in the corridor and hearing me scream in agony she walked up to them and in a very stern voice said, "No you will not". I can hear her voice as she repeated this to me because all my life, she had stood up for herself, and the good of others. Ronda Bird-Parker calls this Immediate Obedience when God's voice comes out and everyone must obey, the Holy Spirit saved me. Luckily, they had just started letting people visit because covid had calmed down, I was so grateful that my mother was there and able to protect me.

My mother is another earth angel, who was told to go and be there to intervene when they could have broken my spinal cord and I could have been in a wheelchair for the rest of my life.

If they had put me in a hoist, my back would have crumbled and been even worse than it was. My mother protected me and was there for me in a holy instant as my teacher Gabby Bernstein would call it.

The doctors came into the X-ray room to watch me still pushing and gathering up the strength to get back on the bed. Finally, I managed to reach the top of the bed and I laid on my tummy in agony. Naked under my hospital gown, I felt terrified, vulnerable and weak as my body was shaking, they gave me more and more morphine which felt like it did nothing. I felt like I was in a very slow death being punished with a cancer that was trying to take over. I was diagnosed with a very rare incurable cancer called Multiple Myeloma which is more common in elderly people. I had legions all

Protected Awakenings

over my back setting into my bones and that's why I was getting weaker.

A few days later the results came in from the MRI scan. I found out that I had broken my back in three places. I say that I broke my back, but to be honest the way the nurses helped me get up, I then realised it was every fall that made a fracture. Every time I stood up. I was making more fractures daily. my bones were so weak even sitting up was too much for me.

The storm (my cancer) had destroyed my bones. After fainting on nurses and them putting me back in bed several times by my arms and legs they were constantly pumping me with more morphine, I realised that being in a general hospital with no specialists meant I wasn't really being cared for. My first fall was when I asked to go to the toilet, and I fainted over a frame even though I couldn't sit up let alone get out of bed with a broken back. I remember waking up to several people holding me by my arms and legs putting me back in bed and feeling like I had fallen from a building. The second fall was in the X-ray room. At one point they told me that I should have a blood transfusion and I said no the second time I think they asked my family, and I had an awakening that I really really was dying, I had given up.

This was when I thought I had had a great life, I travelled the world, I fell in love, real love, I manifested a trip to the Maldives. I went snorkelling with sea turtles, I taught children, I gave back the same skill I learnt and loved as a child, I had lived a great life. My body was done, and it was time to go. I was ready. I was willing to give up. I find it hard

The Storm

to explain this moment, but I know it was the end because my body was caving in on itself.

The doctors told my family that I had about five years left, thinking that was the end also. The moment I agreed to the blood transfusion which my dad had told me I should really have; I had a rebirth. I died and came back the next day with hives all over me because I was allergic to the blood. I only remember opening my eyes to the other side of hell. I was protected, if you have read this far you have seen some of my darkest alleys and I want to say thank you that you braved it with me because me telling you all this is harder than going to therapy.

I was held and guided and the awakenings I had before I went into hospital were strong, I was studying my own spiritual scary part of facing the storm and I had seen examples of hanging on, pulling through and crying through the pain. I lay there thinking not all storms come to disrupt your life some storms come to clear the path. The blood transfusion cleared my blood, cleared my blood cancer and cleared the path.

Maybe you too have been through a storm not as bad as mine, a traumatic event or just a moment where the chaos absorbed you completely and you saw only red. I want you to know not to give into negativity, stay still in the eye of the storm and you will be guided if you do see one coming. I realise that we all have an internal struggle. Sometimes it's in us and, sometimes it's outside of us, but just know that God/ The Universe will hold you through this internal struggle. The Universe wants you to be the mountain that doesn't move, doesn't change, just watches the weather as it goes through another season.

Like the cover of this book, The Angel falls in Venezuela, it does not change, it does not fall, whenever there is a storm the water flows and the ginormous power of God stays still.

Philippians 4:7: "And the peace of God, which transcends all understanding, will guard your heart and minds in Christ Jesus."

The moon is going through another phase while you heal and deal with many emotions. Give these over and watch as the storm passes because you are stronger than the storm and your future self will thank you later.

When there is a storm we look externally, we look for a way to escape the moment and a quick getaway. We look for the space where there is not a problem, and this is wrong. We ignore our intuition which is screaming at us.

"If you have a problem the best thing to do is go in."—*Sean G Murphy*

Look in the eye of the storm, that is where the problem lies. In my case that was the day my gut instinct screamed, and I gave up and said, no, this one is not for me to sort out. God, I surrender.

When Ronda said, just say: ***"GOD HOLD MY HAND"***—***Ronda Bird-Parker***

I gave it to God each time I was in pain, and I said please take this storm because I cannot take it.

The Storm

When I lay on the bathroom floor in agony, I knew there was a problem inside of me. The storm was leading me to the highest good to get the cancer out.

The storm, my cancer, was spreading and getting worse. If I never went to hospital, I would not have been able to write this book for you today. I don't drink or smoke and I have mostly looked after my body. I have eaten healthily, but my diet and weight would always yo-yo up and down depending on my mood and hormones.

In the process of being protected you must trust that even through the storm you will remain strong, let the storm pass through you to reach the other side.

Whatever your storm is, we all have a storm, and if you are seeing a storm remember it cannot last forever the rain has to clear and that rainbow will appear out of nowhere. These are the days that make you stronger.

Another quote I used to see and hear that helped me a lot is by a student of Sean G Murphy.

This too shall pass! - @longliveneno

Another mentor called Neno; who I watch online would repeat this over and over for those of us watching hard times unfold in front of us. Too see his call and Instagram page go to @longliveneno

"You're the mountain watching the storm."—Sean G Murphy

Protected Awakenings

Just like the quote I saw that morning, this storm did not come to ruin my life, it came to save my life. When you think everything is going wrong, God and the angels are protecting you. Don't look at every disruption like it's the end of the world, it's not. They are protecting you. Every day you wake up, a united gathering of invisible guardians are making sure you don't get knocked down crossing the road and you're crying that you didn't get that job interview. Go through that storm, it's an illusion, trust me.

Three steps to approaching a storm, whatever it is, a divorce, a health issue, any kind of trauma, I want to help you and thank you for reading through the hardest time of my life.

Protected Lesson - Step 1
Recognise the storm

Not all storms are scary, you are protected through all of them, there have been other moments in my life when I was filled with anxiety, always running away from facing the problem head on. Brace yourself before any kind of trauma, hold on tight and go in, instead of running away. The enemy (negativity) the outside energy is scared if you focus on the eye of the storm.

As an example, when you watch a children's film and a tiny character kills a dragon or a monster, there is always a character who plucks up the courage to throw the sword into the dragon's eye. That's the kind of focus you must have with the storm that is scaring you.

The Storm

Focus on what needs healing. Put light towards it. Or tell yourself that it's going to be ok, and it will be over soon because you are in charge not the storm. Don't let it overwhelm you because believe me, it could get worse.

Focus on the eye of the storm and not the chaos, in my story my focus was the pain. I knew I had to get the cancer out of me, and I knew it was dangerous. Now I know why the enemy was trying to distract me all the time, to try to kill me with nightmares to try distracting me and get in my head.

What storms have you faced and how did you not get caught up in the chaos?

Write them here, don't think just write......

1. What do you do to stay centered?
2. What tools do you have to stay grounded?
3. Write without thinking, what makes you feel protected?

_____

_____

_____

Is it God?

Is it meditation?

Is it the universe and the earth that grounds you?

Protected Awakenings

In case you're not sure yet that is ok too...

Whatever it is, hold on to it and let it protect you in a spiritual bubble and keep the bubble around you because when the storm comes it will try to search you, your body, your mind and look at how to tear you down. All the energy the enemy sees in you and around you. He took my love, my life, my good health all in the blink of an eye. When he saw I lost my connection to God he smiled and swept in to take over like you see in a tornado. I now feel like the aftermath of a hurricane, the broken trees and the ripped apart houses are my soul. As I open up to you in this chapter, I really feel God is rebuilding me. But you must notice everything, all the red flags, and call out to recognise the storm whatever that is for you; the divorce, the breakup, the trauma, the pain, the health issue as we all have some kind of trauma in our lives, whether it's big or small let go of all that happened and practise centring yourself in God/The Universe to save your soul from drifting into the unknown.

Broken things can become blessed things if you let God do the mending.—unknown

Protected Lesson - Step 2
This too shall pass!

I heard this on Neno's call, his podcasts are amazing. Your angels are holding you while you go through hell, they are waiting and praying for you while you go through it, distracted by chaos. In my situation Ronda told me to hold God's hand. The Universe wants you to be held in the arms of love. In this holding you must go through the lion's Den

The Storm

like Daniel did in the bible. Hold on to your faith. Don't stop in chaos, there is nothing there for you, keep moving and remember **this too shall pass.** What is happening now is not only your story. There are many people still stuck in the storm and they are stuck in a circle unable to see who is weak and who is strong. As we get tested every day, look at the enemy and say, I am the mountain made for all weather. The calm not just before the storm but throughout the whole storm.

I even got a temporary tattoo that said this too shall pass for my treatments. This saying can be used in all circumstances and perspectives. I'm so thankful that nothing lasts forever.

Protected Lesson - Step 3
Be open with your heart first

Before I show you how to open your heart, please remember this is what I believe, and you don't have to believe in what I believe in. Just please be open minded to my concepts. Accept that a higher power wants to help you. When you open up then the light can take all the darkness away from you. You were not meant to hang on to the darkness, sadness, pain, grief, depression, anxiety or fear.

You were not born an angry baby. A higher power held you and decided who you were going to be before you were even born. A higher power held you and said you are meant to be here, and I want you to have an abundance in your heart and in your life, that is your true self, sitting in love, being in love with life and pouring that on to others, for the

Protected Awakenings

God/Universe needs you to be the light. There is enough darkness and evil in the world, don't be a part of that, we all have freedom of choice so choose to be what you were really born into. You can break free anytime, any day, I know you have to be brave to visualise the peace after the storm but it's always waiting for you.

I do believe that God promised us that, when Jesus was crucified, we would find peace after the storm. Now we don't have to suffer.

I believe Jesus took all our pain and suffering for us and died and rose again so that we could be awakened the same way through him.

I do believe I must be open to Jesus helping me If I want him in my life, in my awakenings and any desires of my heart, for God cannot help me if I have a closed fist. You may have another belief, and you don't connect to my relationship with Jesus Christ. Open your heart to the idea that every minute of your life the Universe is working on your behalf to make life work out for you. As I write this book, I surrender to God/the universe every day and I give everything over so that I receive more blessings than before.

Opening your heart can be hard so I have created this prayer for you.

You may find this tricky, but the more you practise it, the better it will feel.

Practise opening your heart to this heart exercise I'm about to show you, I have also spoken about in another

The Storm

book I'm in by David Poole called **Heartset – Your key to a limitless Mindset.The subtitle is, The antidote to painful Quantum Leaps.**

I have co-authored the book I have named above with some amazing mentors and coaches.

Here is how I practise breathing into my heart and opening up. Follow me in this simple practice, do it every time you feel panic, anxiety and worry. Think about holding your heart and mind in peace and staying there.

Breathe in and take notice of your breath
Breathe in for four
Hold your breath for four
Breathe out for four

There are many breathing techniques you can do, one that helped me a lot when I was having panic attacks was breathing in the shape of a square. Imagine your finger drawing a square. Imagine drawing up one side of the square and breathe in slowly for four seconds, then breathe out for six seconds, breathe in for four seconds down then across breathe out for six seconds across and you have completed the square as shown below.

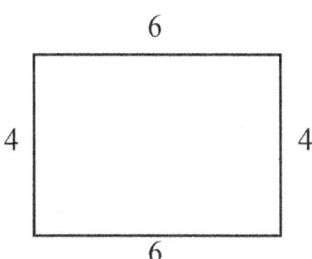

Protected Awakenings

It is believed that your brain can't concentrate on the numbers while in fight or flight mode, and it grounds you by calming your breathing down.

You could also do this and imagine breathing from the centre of your heart.

To help you to breathe into your heart read this prayer, write it down, highlight it and makes notes afterwards here or in a journal.

God/Universe/Angels

I open up now to you as you hold me, find me, search me, uplift me and heal me as I breathe into your presence and faith that you will always surround me in an invisible love around my heart. My true nature. Open my eyes to the heart you made and make me see what serves me the most as I gaze into the eyes of the blessings you made only for me. Like the fingerprint you gave me that only I have, thank you for giving me this peace I feel within my body that my heart is held by you today and every day. Breathe into me as I breathe into you, I choose to be open, and I open my palms out to you.

As soon as you do this practice you are acknowledging the heart that God or the Universe gave you and the heart that wants to be itself (your true self).

A heart that wants love, feels love looks for love and follows love.

The Storm

God is the same, it wants to support you, love you and hold you.

Do this practice daily and watch your vibration change as you tell your heart you are in a safe space and your heart is heard as God/Universe is always listening and waiting for you to open up.

Your heart is connecting to your breath and feeling it.

Open your heart and let the light in! Let God/Universe in and if you're really brave connect to God and say thank you for my breath and the oxygen always supporting my heart.

Protected Lesson

Picture the peace, close your eyes and think about it, visualise it

What was the lesson from the storm?

Once God/The Universe/Angels can see that you acknowledge the lesson or the bigger reason for the storm, they will see you're ready to let go of it and they will take what you can't handle.

When we see the lessons and we learn from the storm, the lesson will not repeat again. This is when we are spiritually growing.

You are always protected from the storm through the storm and even when the storm is over.

Protected Awakenings

Keep surrendering to the angels and they will give you all you need for the path unknown to you that is ahead of you.

I know it's hard to visualize the peace after the storm when you're in the middle of it. The song 'Somewhere over the rainbow' comes to mind. Keep this inside you, we all hear the saying that time heals everything and its true it really does.

Say this prayer:

God, please hold me while I go through my own chaos (give over your storm here or write it down), this place that I should not be in. Hold my true vision and my pure heart for I want this to pass and I want to learn the lesson, so I never see it again, so it never repeats_____(to who you believe in). Hold me in the love and light that you truly want me to see. Give me the perfect solution and give me vision to see the peace and the true picture of peace and harmony after the storm, that I am love and I spread only your light with you by my side.

Once you do this and say this you are being stronger than half the population.

"I'll see it when I believe it."—DR. WAYNE DYER

2 Corinthians 5:7
For we live by faith and not by sight

This bible verse has always stayed with me. Some storms I ignored and now I see that the more we visualise a positive outcome and give it to God, the more he will take it for you,

The Storm

but you also have to do the work and visualise the peace you're praying for all the time.

This must be the hardest chapter I have ever told anyone. Thank you for staying with me through what I perceive as the moments where I thought I failed in my life but only made me stronger. I myself could cry from all I have written here, but I want you to know that when we share, let go, let our hearts break in the truth of what happened, then we are closer to healing, telling a friend, opening up about that storm that time you closed up and you got scared it's ok to talk about it, write about it like I have in many journals I now stare at like the covers of a horror story. God got me out and the universe lead me back to God and you can do this with any situation in your life, so remember these steps I given you.

Recognise the storm, see that it's coming like when countries get ready for a hurricane. Remember, this too shall pass, and then picture the peace and you will be fine, you are stronger than you think, or you will ever know. If no one told you today then God, the Universe and all those you cannot see yet or have never heard of (the angels) love you today, yesterday and forever.

CHAPTER 7
Dressed in White

I came out of hospital after being there for a month, I got in the shower and started a conversation with God all in my mind. I was thinking about how my illness was all my fault and how I didn't look after myself. My negative self-talk was creeping in, with all my quick-firing questions, there were also quick answers in my mind. Every time I got in the shower my thoughts would drift between what my higher self said and what my negative self-talk said. At this point my initial thought that kept clinging to me was *"Lord I need a sign"*. I know I have cancer and it's all my fault. Thinking to myself you're punishing me. He replied very quickly, and I heard It's not your fault. I started to get annoyed with my higher self or God I wasn't so sure. I loudly and angrily fought back in my mind. Like a huge argument was going on and I was watching. It is my fault, and I can't undo this situation, **I need a sign**.

Now before you think I had lost the plot I stepped out of the shower determined that my ego was right.

Protected Awakenings

In my head I said I need to see someone wearing all white God please and only then will I believe it's not my fault.

I was convinced I would not even see the colour white all day. I was angry at God because I felt like I didn't listen to him.

My dad said we had to hurry to the hospital because I had an appointment for a review of my medication and an update on my progress with my progress with my treatment plan.

As I sat in my dad's car, I stared vacantly at people walking on the streets, everyone wearing black and just going about their normal day. I won't get my sign I thought, I didn't look after myself and I was burnt out and I just so happen to have a rare cancer that would limit my life, I thought.

I waited at the pharmacy on my own for my prescription and I went on Sean's daily awakening call, listening to the wisdom and the message for the day. I looked up and there standing in front of me was a **white** man. He was wearing a **white** puffer jacket, he looked like he was in his late 70s, he was wearing **white** trousers, he had **white** trainers he even had **white** socks and his hair was **white** and suited him so much, my jaw dropped to the floor. **God had given me my sign.** It wasn't my fault. I repeated to myself maybe it wasn't my fault.

I was so shocked I got my sign. I wish someone took a picture of me. I didn't know where to look, what to say or how to feel, all I knew was God was real, God was listening, and he had listened to me and my strange conversation I had with him in the shower. I couldn't make it up. I was literally shouting at myself in my head in the morning and in

Dressed in White

the space of two-three hours the sign I asked for (someone **dressed in white**) was staring at me like a deer in headlights. I was in awe of God and how he listened, and it wasn't my fault and I needed to stop beating myself up.

Feeling so strange yet happy loved and speechless at the same time, I walked back to my dad, got in the car and was shell shocked all the way home that I actually got my sign. You too can ask for a sign. I want to help you do this and to be in awe of the world you are in right now. Witness how God/The Universe and everything is moving around for you. You are one chess piece on the board, don't ever think you're just going to lose the game every time. Think about how the moon moves round while you sleep, the world is moving at such a fast pace but imagine if I told you that everyone in this world is being protected and only some of them know it. If you picked up this book and you have read this far, I want you to open to a presence that wants to show you how much it cares for you and wants to show you again and again for the rest of your life. Because you are more precious than anything else and your every step is being watched I hope and pray that you follow that sign that says your life is this way and feel even more guided.

You can have a constant dialogue with the universe like you are texting a friend. God/the Universe knows what's in your heart and wants to hear what's troubling you. Tell him, the universe is always listening, and you don't have to even say a word.

Sometimes when we are in a full conversation with God, we realise that we think that relying on our own strength and overthinking everything we can think ourselves out of a situation. This is not true the mindset that you're stuck in is not the mindset that will get you out and free you.

When I asked for a sign, I thought that I was proving that angels, the universe and all the things I was reading and learning about, were not true.

I wanted to believe in the same fear-based story we all believe in, that we live in a cold world where no one cares about us. This is a lie; we are always protected.

If you ask God to show you a sign or you pray and the answer to your prayer comes to you super-fast then don't be surprised. I have written my prayers down and I have said them in my mind too. Prepare for what you have prayed for because when you are honest in your heart that you need an answer the answers make you feel a presence that was there since you were born, however no one explained this presence or took the time to help you understand why you would need to feel more protected. This presence is for you from God himself.

I will guide you now in these three steps to ask for a sign and connect the best way you can.

Protected Lesson - Step 1
Speak to the universe

I asked for a man in white and then God proved to me that it wasn't my fault and that my journey has a higher purpose.

Dressed in White

When asking for a sign you can ask for anything it could be a noise, a knowing, a bird, you can ask in meditation. You can ask for an animal or a number or even something you very rarely see.

I asked for a sign, and I got nothing which is also a message. If you don't get your sign, it's not meant for you. Ask and then let it go, ask for help, you can't know everything all on your own, give it over.

Say this prayer...

If you want to write this down to think more clearly you are more than welcome to do what feels right for you. Or say this in your mind.

God/Universe/Angels, to who I believe in...

Please show me a sign, I would like to see _____ (fill in the blank)

To whom I believe in......... please make it clear to me, prove to me that your pathway is greater than the crossroads I think I should be standing at.

As soon as you say this prayer, let it go. Imagine that you have just posted a letter in a post box, and you know it has been delivered already. Once you let it go you have given the universe a clear indication that you are ready and prepared for when it comes. If the sign does not come, then the Universe is preparing you for it. If you don't see it at all then it's a sign that what you're asking for is not for you right now, ask for the highest good for you want what is in

Protected Awakenings

alignment with you because the Universe knows the best plan for you more than you do.

Protected Lesson - Step 2
Prepare for what you pray for

Sometimes we pray as though it's never on the way. The more you let go the more your blessings come to you faster. The universe does not like needy energy. I once stood waiting in a long queue for my coffee in Starbucks and I saw this quote on Instagram and I said thank you, thank you, thank you that I get to enjoy this coffee now and instantly thought about how I wanted to journal that day and change my thoughts from what I wanted, and my coffee came instantly. Think about the universe in the same way. Tell God/The Universe everything and think about what you would do if you got all your signs today, how would you celebrate and acknowledge that a higher power heard you?

See yourself jumping for joy excited that God is with you in the happiness he created for you.

Don't beg angels who are holding you up every day and who planned the whole day for you. Your angels are working, just as hard as you. They are on your side, hoping, praying and waiting for you to find the missing piece of the puzzle that everything you need is within you. The answers to all your questions are inside of you, you just haven't opened yourself up yet. The wisdom in you is more than you realise. Look within and you must prepare for what you are praying for.

Dressed in White

In my story I was not prepared and then I was in complete shock when I got my prayer answered because when you don't trust the universe, you're blocking your blessings.

God/Universe/Angels, make miracles every day and what we find fascinating is normal to them, they have more in store for you.

Each day God helps people, he gives people their prayers and it gives everyone something they have been longing for, for years. Ask God to guide you and you will be amazed.

Protected Lesson - Step 3
Say Thank you

When you thank God/The Universe for more answers, signs and synchronicities happen. For the past seventeen months I have been practising gratitude and saying thank you for the things I pray for and more and more of my desires have come true.

Life flows where your attention goes, life flows where it is meant to be. You are meant to know about your true self.

You are meant to know that you are loved, led by light and that your true spirit (your true self) within you is love too, and who you really are and who you are supposed to be is light and free. Free from worry and anxiety.

Being in gratitude lead me to so many beautiful pathways.

Protected Awakenings

Say thank you for all the awakenings and light-bulb moments and times the penny dropped when you thought, you know what? I think I'm going to be alright. Say thank you. For that time and the time before and how you are still alive today! Say Thank you.

This feeling is love, this feeling is your guardian angel relaxing, saying thank God, look my work here is done.

Say this prayer with me...

My Universe / My God / To all the angels before me...

Thank you for always guiding me and always letting me see a glimmer of hope to lead me to my next chapter, the next sign that you make for me to walk the right path into the light, that is out of this darkness, I thank you that continue to have more awareness while I open up to you now and always. Thank you that my sign is in your hands and that only you have the power to let me know I am always going the right way by following and being aware of you.

Ask for an answer and speak to God as though you are speaking to your best friend. Prepare for what you prayed for and then be thankful for what you asked for knowing it's on the way. Remember if you don't see it. You are not quite ready for it or you have something better coming your way. Remember that your path is always preparing you. Always be thankful in the process.

CHAPTER 8
The angel in my intuition

In 2015, I went on a night out with my best friends from high school. I was so excited to have a dance and be with them. On the dance floor I was in my element, showing off because dancing is my first love. My friend Sarah asked me, shouting over the music, "Who do you like in here?" I said, "The guy behind you at 12 o'clock and don't look now you will make it obvious." Sarah looked and said, "I'm going to tell him". She walked straight up to the guy in the crowded club. The room was very small, and it was getting busy as she ran over to tell him. When she got back the guy smiled at me excitedly. Sarah looked at me and I laughed. "That's the wrong guy" I said, now feeling so embarrassed. Sarah laughed at me too with a cheeky look on her face and drinking her drink with a straw, tilting her head to the side. I told her I liked the guy that was behind him. I got a lot of attention from guys at that time, and I started to become really picky about who I let into my world, so I found it even more funny that suddenly my friends were having fun

Protected Awakenings

annoying me. I was so in love with my ex, and I was deeply upset when it fizzled out and I was scared to be with anyone who wasn't the same as the love I had. Sarah said, "ok tell me what he looks like." Feeling grateful that she wanted to be my wing woman I looked and describe this tall, gorgeous guy laughing with his friends. She swiftly disappeared to talk to him.

He walked over and I instantly had butterflies in my tummy. He asked me if I wanted a drink and I said yes, and we walked over to the bar. Then we both went outside as we couldn't hear each other over the blaring music in our ears.

Outside he asked me where I was from and where I lived only to find out that he lived 15 minutes away from me. Nicholas and I just clicked instantly, conversation flowed effortlessly, and his smile was infectious. The positive energy radiated from him completely.

We talked some more, and he left his friends and drove me home. I was completely in disbelief that I met someone new, so amazing, so quickly. He really was the breath of fresh air I really wanted.

At this point in my life, I was happy with everything I had going for me. I had a great job teaching swimming, I was happy in my body and had been working out every day, I was on a great path to manifesting my desires and creating the life I knew I wanted. My hair was growing, it was sunny all the time for summer which was rare in London and people at work would always ask me if I was seeing anyone and I always said no.

The angel in my intuition

After I met Nick that night we went out on a date, and we spent lots of time together. We went to the gym together and we became very close. But a few months before I met Nick, I had been manifesting a job to work abroad as a swim teacher.

Nick and I were together for about six months, not officially, but we were really aligned with our lives and spent as much time together as we could.

In April 2016, I had to tell him I was going abroad, and I asked God how I was going to do that. How am I going to tell this guy that I like so much that I'm leaving the UK? I was in pieces. This guy felt like the one and I had to leave him. It was like I manifested what I wanted, but not all the parts in between.

I flew to Ibiza to become a swimming teacher at an all-inclusive hotel, and I cried on the plane. Was this what I wanted? Would everything be, ok? Would I like it there? How will I feel? So many questions filled my mind while the plane took off and I finally felt free.

In 2020, I was in bed, not feeling well after all the chemo and steroids I had been on. Feeling the energy of the world changing because of the pandemic. Not realising that my intuition, the feelings and power in me, had changed. All the meditations I had taken were making me stronger and was changing me and all the awakenings I was having everyday were shifting my feelings faster than I realised.

Something was nagging at me and pulling me every day. I listened and I thought about Nick time and time again.

Protected Awakenings

I felt something was wrong with him. My first thought was, is he sick? Does he have covid? I asked God and I heard, no, he needs you to call him.

I followed that feeling, I called him, no reply all day, I asked God, what do I do now? I felt as though God was saying call him, I said I did, and then I heard, text him, I texted him over and over. He finally replied and I felt more and more anxious.

This nagging urgent feeling consumed me. I asked my intuition, what's wrong? I asked God is it his family? And God said, no. No more replies, just a nagging like a child pulling at my clothes wherever I went.

Saturday the 31st of July 2021, he messaged me and said, "Hey, what made you message me so late last night?". I explained how I had been following my intuition and he said, "Well, you were right," and said he had a lot going on.

I felt the need to really listen and be there for him.

Nick said, "You're not the only one who has checked on me, my ex-girlfriend also texted me saying she didn't know what was going on with me, but God told her to pray for me".

My heart opened in disbelief; my eyes widened as I read the text that the nagging I followed was right all along.

Nicholas got the news that he was a father, however, he found out in the worst way when the child was already a year old. After doing a paternity test it was confirmed and from what he told me I knew he felt vulnerable just sharing the story with me. I knew at this point that he felt low, depressed

The angel in my intuition

and disappointed. I told him how proud I was of him for handling the situation and the blessing it is to have a child that so many out there have never been able to experience and I knew God wanted me to help change his perspective on what was happening.

While I did this, I was thanking God that he was not sick and that he was ok and completely protected by those around him.

Protected Lesson.
Never Ignore your intuition this is for you and me. It's your guardian angel, we are all being used as a part of the puzzle to be a part of God's plan. I was being asked to check on Nicholas and also his other ex-girlfriend was praying too. We are all being used as someone else's angel. I followed my gut instinct even when my ego told me I was stressing about nothing, I followed God's calling to check on him.

Our guardian angels can be our gut instinct and they know that something is not quite right. I now see these as warnings in bright yellow. Listen to your body when it's talking to you, saying, hello, over here, come and listen to me.

Some days we are angels for others because God needs us to serve and be there for others.

We question when we have a gut feeling if it is real or not. Believe me I have had this feeling many times and it has never let me down. Don't think you were just wondering, it's more than that. Remember a gut feeling could save a life, or in my story help someone in need.

In my story my gut instinct knew something was wrong which was my cancer, and I knew I had to go to hospital. Imagine if I didn't go, I wouldn't be alive.

Your gut feeling is there to protect you and others. We always look externally at everything. Instead, we should always look within and ask the question.

If everything we need is inside of us, then all we must discover the intelligence that's already there.

These three steps will help you to listen to the power you have. Look after that power and follow your intuition even when you think it doesn't mean anything.

Protected Lesson - Step 1
Ask God/the Universe how can I serve today?

We are angels for others every day. We must ask what can I do to help today?

When you wake up in the morning ask this question.

Say this to yourself or write it down in a journal...

Dear God/The Universe

Use me to serve others for I want to share my light and love to help other people and be part of the highest good for all. Let me follow my intuition to text my friend who is in need of prayer right now,

The angel in my intuition

to serve someone who wants to hear God's voice through me.

Sometimes you feel compelled to text that person who is on your mind is not just a coincidence. My mentor Sean G Murphy calls it a *(Godcidence) God plus coincidence (Godcidence) another way of saying meant to be.*

Psychology explains that when you think of someone, half the time they are thinking about you too. This is a psychological fact.

What if I told you God/The Universe has made you think about someone on purpose to text them before they do something they will regret or text them just before they get into trouble.

It's simple just ask God how do I serve today? You will be amazed at how much you can help.

Protected Lesson - Step 2
Follow your heart

Follow your heart and follow your gut, people say all the time. We spend so much time in our heads and not thinking with our hearts and our heart misses us.

Follow the knowing I choose to follow daily. Make it a daily commitment to think with your heart. The same calling, I got to message Nicholas and to go to hospital on my own, God wanted me to help, with more love.

Protected Awakenings

We are all like ants in a jungle helping each other to build a nest. Your small acts of kindness make this world a better place.

Often, I have helped people, I have given my book to a homeless person or given in a way no one expected. I have told a girl she looks beautiful in a dress. I have stepped out of my comfort zone to make someone's day and sit in my heart and connect to theirs. For one small act of kindness can remind someone that they are not alone, they are loved and that you have noticed and seen them.

Protected Lesson - Step 3
Trust your inner self

Trust that everything you need is inside of you. You are protected even inside yourself and your heart. Your body knows when you need rest, when you need water and when you are hungry. Keep Listening.

Your body knows when something is wrong with you and when you're not taking care of yourself.

Trust that even if you cannot work out what you need right now, your intuition will kick in and work for you on its own because the nagging doesn't stop, and the Universe will show you. God will tell you; I now realise that everything has a sign and a connection. It's there for you to connect the dots and follow it. Trust your inner knowing and inner being that's guiding you now, today, tomorrow to your higher self.

The angel in my intuition

Say this Prayer

God / Universe

I Trust that God within me is listening as I pray to my own inner wisdom. I know that everything I need I already have within me and that I can feel and understand when my intuition talks to me, give me my own personal gift to understand how to trust you, listen as I serve myself to look after myself and others all for the highest good, for you know it all. (To who you believe in).

You must ask God first, question it, what is wrong? Journal your thoughts and prayers that you learn in this book remember that this is a practice and a process.

_____

_____

_____

_____

_____

_____

_____

_____

_____

Protected Awakenings

Follow your heart and your intuition together. Follow and recognise that you know the answer inside of you. Once you have done this, trust the answer is inside of you. That you already know and will be open to it. Once you have done this, The answer will come, and pray to your inner wisdom for all the answers you will hear in your own silence and remember your guardian angel is inside of you. If you feel this is a tricky step, ask God / The universe to speak to you so loudly that you know who it is and trust that it's so clear it's the answer you're so glad you got a chance to listen to.

CHAPTER 9
Surrender to all angels

Nicholas said he wanted to see me and go out for dinner, we talked for two hours on the phone, and I told him about how I had cancer and am now in remission. He told me more about becoming a father and we spoke like we were never apart. Writing my gratitude in my journal I was thankful for everything in my life and staying connected to God as much as I could.

I was so nervous to see Nick because I had shaved all my hair off and I looked so different from the girl he met with the long curly hair and full of energy. I was embracing having no hair and my brother reminded me of all the celebs who were always changing their image to make a statement and told me to just go with it. For the first time since 2019 I was going out for dinner since covid restrictions, and I was nervous even though I told myself not to be. I came out of hospital on the 10th of July 2021, so it had been a month since I was home.

Protected Awakenings

After finishing my gratitude journaling, I put on YouTube and found an Ibiza playlist of all the music from the summer before and I started to write ...

Dear angels

I surrender to you, and I give everything over to you.

As I was finishing the sentence a song made me stop completely. A song came on called 'Surrender' by *Jorm & Ludvigsson (Feat. Thomas Daniel)*

I had never heard the song before, and I was listening to the lyrics more and more. It mentions a battleground and surrendering.

Tears ran down my face as I realised that I was being spoken to through music, I felt a presence I had felt before. The unbreakable love of the God and all the angels, I had surrendered to was cloaking me in joy and love which reassured me that they were listening and always there, and that I should go and live my life without fear.

I didn't know the song, but I knew it was an angel.

God was comforting me, he wanted me to see Nicholas and I felt I had to help him too.

I couldn't believe I had just written **I surrender to all angels** *and a song came on called* **I surrender**, *and I had never listened to this playlist before, my life felt like a movie.*

Surrender to all angels

I felt emotional and a wave of happiness rushed over me as Nick texted me saying he was running late, but he was on his way.

<u>Protected Lesson</u> *– Surrender, let go and everything will come to you. The more you surrender and acknowledge the angels working, your life will happen with more flow as it's supposed to for the highest good. Remember you are an ant in the jungle of spirituality, and you help those who are there to help you because we are all serving God/The Universe together so surrender and watch the miracles unfold.*

That evening I met Nicholas and it felt as if we had never been apart as though I was never ill. I felt so aligned to be with someone who knew me before I was ill and when I was happy in my true self before the world took away my dreams and tried to tell me to live in fear.

We sometimes think that no one is listening. We go about our daily lives thinking that we are all alone, and that no one cares about us, all the lies we tell ourselves that miracles never happen or are very rare even though Jesus performed miracles all the time, but we think that's only in an old book. Everything we witness is a miracle, me writing this book now is a miracle in itself.

We rely on our own thinking that we must nag and nag when we pray. What if you listened and surrendered instead?

Write down how you really feel. Write down your surrender moments, what's bothering you and what is holding you back?

Hand it over, when you're being protected, how can you protect what you have if you don't give it to a higher power?

With these three steps I will show you how I surrendered so that you can too.

"When we surrender, we should surrender some more."— Gabby Bernstein"

Do this practice with me to act even when you're not sure. Tell the angels you surrender to them and ask God to hold what you're not sure about and watch miracles happen that have always been waiting for you.

Albert Einstein said "There are only two ways to live your life. One is as though nothing is a miracle; the other is as though everything is a miracle"

Protected Lesson - Step 1
Hand it over!

In Chapter 4 I mentioned how to surrender. This is a daily practice you must commit to here and I can give you another chance to do it again.

Imagine you are physically handing it over this time. Sit down and journal how you really feel. Remember surrendering is about being honest and really letting go. God

Surrender to all angels

(who you believe in) knows what you need. Remember God has a plan greater than yours.

This time write to the angels and see what they show you, you can do this and imagine you're talking to Siri or Alexa.

Every night before you go to sleep and every time you wake up in the morning say this mantra.

God/Universe/Angels I want to see before me

I give this to you, for I know you have the best way to the solution better than mine.

_____

_____

_____

Protected Lesson - Step 2
Listen, even the radio knows your favourite song

Listen, watch and look around you, God knows your hearts deepest desires. God knows which blessings are coming to you and the exact time you need them.

When you hand over the insecurities again and again the angels will handle what you cannot. Then the Universe or the angels can play a song on the radio when you get in a taxi, God can show you signs and other ways to listen to get your attention. God/the Universe could put that book in a shop window that you walk past that will change your life or give you the solution to something that you couldn't do yourself.

Protected Lesson - Step 3
<u>Follow the highest good</u>

Remember to ask for the highest good. Daily God and the Universe work hand-in-hand with angels to help you. If it's not for the highest good, it won't happen. Ask that God takes care of you and of others and watch everything just fall into place.

Surrender again and again and again, *Hand it over, listen because even the radio is talking to you and knows what you may need to hear. Follow the highest good. In the next chapter I will explain how angels can translate so that you understand them even more.*

CHAPTER 10
Angels are Translating

On the 27th of August 2021, I posted a video on my story of a sign that said, please keep your distance and keep social distancing, I zoomed in. The sign also said.

God bless you reading this, **JESUS IS KING!**

A guy from Australia named Alex who had just started following me messaged saying.

Tell me about your relationship with Jesus.

I wrote about my devotional a book my friend had suggested **Jesus calling by Sarah Young.** I explained that I pray even when I hear something I don't like the sound of. I give it to him. God talks to me as well and I follow whatever I feel he is trying to tell me to do and to help as much as I can.

Typing this to someone I didn't know very well, felt strange.

I asked Alex about his relationship with Jesus.

Protected Awakenings

Alex said, "it's something that I've started to feel a bit lately. I feel like they encourage me to go after smaller things in the hopes that they will lead to bigger things for me."

I said, "what do you feel?", not really understanding myself. I asked, "what encourages you?"

Alex said, "I think it encourages me to be the best version of myself and to be able to help people. But I don't quite know what they target me with." Alex went on to say.

"I do have feelings like a higher power is recommending I make decisions."

I replied very quickly this time.

Alex referred to a higher power as (It) and I copied what he said even thought this is not how I speak of a higher power.

"It (God) wants you to be the best version of yourself all the time. There are people who help in so many ways. Each of us have a role to play and you can too as it (God) wants to guide you always."

The universe is always listening.

Alex agreed.

"I believe that"

"How long have you believed in Jesus for?"

I explained "Properly since I was about 15."

"Cool" Alex said.

Angels are Translating

That night I told my friend Katerin about this strange conversation I had, and she said yes, you were being channelled.

This was not the first time, but this was the first time I referred to God as (It).

I sat back in my chair, the fact that I told Alex that God was called (it) did not feel right, however, that is how he would understand the message. God is my best friend, my saviour, and my father. He means everything to me and here I was calling him a new name so I could translate and let Alex hear him.

<u>Protected Lesson</u> – God and the angels will use anyone so that you can understand them. They will speak to people who are atheists, people who are not religious at all, people who are not even spiritual. If you don't ask for help the angels can't help you. God and the angels are looking to communicate all the time through more and more love that is all around. The invisible angels want you to see more miracles unfold in your life, even as you read this book, that is my prayer for you, that they translate all the time.

Not everyone believes in God, and I get it, not everyone believes in angels. Angels are constantly translating, changing direction for you, for you to see the signs that you're being guided, followed and always protected. While I write this now, I feel deep in my heart that is my purpose, to share my story and awaken you to something I wanted to believe was true but I didn't see, until the messages were everywhere and

Protected Awakenings

the presence was the warmest feeling I have ever felt. The peace and calm now I would never trade for anything else. Whatever that means for you I hope you find it in this book. A chance to open your eyes, your heart and your mind to the life in front of you.

We are all helping someone smell the coffee and wake up to the fact that this world is for us and loves us every minute of our day. While angels translate for others, understand that I say 'God' while others say 'Universe' and that's ok. Some say God and others talk about their relationship with Jesus. I was brought up in the Anglican Church, however, I have learnt even more about God and my spirituality outside of church with my own teacher in my life experiences in the past two years than ever before. I know there is a presence that really loves me and has loved me all my life. I have loved ones who do not believe in God but believe that the stars, the moon, and creation look after them 'the universe' constantly listening and giving.

We must translate for others when they are anxious, stuck in a mindset of fear or listening to the enemy with no awareness that he is there to keep them in fear. Don't go down the rabbit hole with them, I pray as I see this happening in front of me. Firstly, because they are not my emotions and second because I must give it to a higher power because God knows what they need now. This is a practice and I believe we are all translating hope for one another, when we phone a friend, find another way or get good advice. For me personally the first person I go to before venting on the phone about my problems, is God.

Angels are Translating

In the next three steps I want to help you understand translating as this took me a while to grasp myself.

Protected Lesson - Step 1
Let the angels in

Angels can't help you if you don't ask and tell them what you need help with. God can't help you if you keep pushing all the boats away that he puts there to save you. There is joke about the parable of the drowning man. The story is about a man who is sitting on a roof during a flood and calling out to God for help. God sends him two boats and a helicopter, but he refuses each saying no, thank you, God will save me. When he dies and asks God why he didn't save him, God says, I sent you two boats and a helicopter, and you turned them all down.

I see angels in the same way as the boats. Angels watch us cross the road and get worked up in fear and anxiety complicating life for ourselves instead of letting go. Our angels watch us detour into fear head on because the way we are going is the wrong way. The angels want us to open up to them. In my story Alex is very curious about God and can see that God wants him to help others.

His intuition is right, and he is being called and guided now as we speak. Alex is just one of the people I have helped who needed someone to tell them they are going in the right direction.

Protected Lesson - Step 2
God/Universe can see what is blocking the way

Sometimes we help people, and they don't want to be helped. We believe that we can rely on how strong we are, and the ego says I am ok when it's not. This is when the chaos happens.

In the bible it says "do not lean on your own understanding" your heart is deceitful, your emotions fluctuate and your understanding does not see the overall big picture.

God never lies, God never changes for God knows all, trust in him first.

Be gentle with yourself or others who close themselves off.

Say this prayer

God/Universe please can you take whatever is blocking me from accepting you into my life and realising the fear and anxiety I subconsciously hold.

When you let God know, the angels can work on your behalf.

As an empath I know we cannot save everyone as much as I want to, this is what Jesus did for us so that we could live. So, help all those who really need it and pray they get help today and step out of their own way.

Angels are Translating

Protected Lesson - Step 3
Translate for others

I translated for Alex, that there is a higher power here with us. I let the angels know to help him to understand his connection more and to have a deeper relationship.

I have translated for my brother also that the Universe is always on his side. I always turn to God when I feel uneasy, and I tell the angels I need reassurance and guidance in the right direction.

Sometimes translating means helping someone find their own road to what is good for them.

Translating could mean answering someone's question about spirituality.

Sometimes it's someone asking if you go to church or what do you do to get closer to consciousness. Other times it's just being a friendly ear and listening or comforting someone when they are crying.

You can translate by being helpful to those around you and you don't have to tell them all you believe in; angels will speak to people in the language they understand.

I have told my brother to speak to the universe and ask, **"Universe, please, how can I look at this situation differently."**

Follow these steps to translate for others or for yourself to understand even more.

Protected Awakenings

Practise being open, notice if you're shutting off from God or if others close their mindset to other possibilities. Translate in how other people speak of a higher power and listen as they speak of what spirituality means to them.

CHAPTER 11
Angel Numbers

I studied dance at college when I was 17, always looking for new music and making and creating choreography. One day searching around for more music, I found a video of one of my favourite singers Keyisha Cole. I came across this video of her talking on a chat show. Keyisha explained why she called her album **11:11** and what it means to her. Keyisha explained how she spent time with the rapper and artist Tupac and how he told her she would be famous. She explained how her mother said she was born around the time **11:11** and spoke of the spiritual knowing that she would always be ok.

One day Keyisha was in her house, and she wanted to move house and couldn't find her birth certificate. Worried she had lost it, she found it in her garage after looking at the time which was... yup, you guessed it, **11:11**.

Be prepared to see these numbers forever, after reading this chapter seeing each number is not a coiendance, its a sign just for you.

Protected Awakenings

When I first heard about this, I thought it must just be a coincidence. I never really accepted it happening in my life or have a deeper meaning like it does now.

If you look up the meaning of these numbers, it will say it's to do with new opportunities and new beginnings. Angels want to awaken you to this number and it's the main one that appears and can appear frequently.

During lockdown I would read posts about spirituality and angel numbers, and I constantly saw **11:11**. Every time I saw them, I wondered what it really meant as I was so curious in my heart, thinking could this all be true. It's believed that the numbers mean new beginnings and that you are being awakened and that you should think about what you were thinking about before you saw the numbers and it would manifest as the angels are with you.

As I read more and more about angel numbers, I started seeing the numbers on my phone, on the washing machine, when I got in the car, on the microwave, on the clock, on our old VCR and on receipts when I paid for shopping and in the most bizarre places angel numbers followed me everywhere.

Listening to my mentor, he said to someone who asked him what these numbers meant, that they are like road signs saying you're going the right way.

I felt drawn to this number. As part of my health journey, the doctors explained I would have to freeze my eggs because the chemo would interfere with my body. I had **11** eggs frozen. In total I froze 15 eggs, they told me there

Angel Numbers

were **11** that were ready and 4 that were premature, i knew this was a sign I couldn't believe it. When I had my stem cell treatment, the ward I was in was number **11**. As soon as I was in hospital, I put my songs on shuffle for new music and the song that came on was **'11:11'** from the album 'The night before the morning'. I knew I was in the right place at the right time, and everything was meant to be. God was with me in the room, the angels were holding me through the chemo I hadn't even had yet. The doctors would walk in and talk to me at **11:11** and even the time I found out I was in remission was around **11:11**.

<u>Protected Lesson</u> - When you see angel numbers think of all the things you need to let go of. Surrender it, remember, seeing numbers means all angels are around you, awakening you, supporting you, loving you, waiting for you to discover yourself. God has sent them for you to be held, be aware when the numbers are around you.

The day I heard the song 'surrender' Nicholas was a angel for me and that was the same day we went out for dinner. I only realised the day after it was the **11**th of august. I only remembered because I made a playlist with the song surrender with the date **11/08/2021**

I have waited in the waiting area to see a consultant to see the weather appear on a tv screen saying it's **11** degrees outside. I have done Gabby Bernstein's meditations for protection before leaving the house and before I go to bed. I have seen the number **11** constantly even though my favourite number is 10. The number **11** even showed up

Protected Awakenings

when taking a ticket for the queue to have a blood test done and when a doctor says can I come back on the 11th of the month, I always say yes.

God is always guiding you with numbers, signs, songs and messages that people are there to help you whenever you ask.

We think we are alone in this world, but we don't know all the realms we don't see.

Angels are amongst us, not just in numbers but in so many ways, keep your eyes open. God wants us to know how loved we are and how loved we have always been, since we were born.

We pass so many miracles that we think they are just good things that happened to us. We must see that these doors are always being opened for us. Be thankful for the numbers you see that you're being supported, even the time you wake up is a sign. Start to notice if you see numbers in the same order, like a code, write them down, it's a message.

These three steps will make you more aware of the protection all around you and numbers speaking to you.

Angel Numbers

Protected Lesson - Step 1
Pay attention to the numbers you see

You might see the same numbers on the phone that are staring at you, on the washing machine and everywhere you go. Notice how you are feeling at that time, look up what the numbers means and write them down.

When I see **11:11**, I know I am being protected and guided or I'm exactly where I need to be. That road sign that says you're going the right way is beneficial because when you have a moment of self-doubt they seem to appear.

Notice the numbers as the message you get will either surprise you or support you so much, it's what you needed today.

Be open to all messages that you're being given, something you never expected on your journey.

Notice the number for a week, are they in sequence? Do you see 111, 222, 333, 444 and how many times at the same time or three days a week, then it's a message that you are being called to see. I keep my Angel number book by Kyle Gray very close at hand so that I can check them.

"Angels are real. I had to start out by saying that, although you probably know it already."—Kyle Gray

Recently I started seeing the number 117 over and over. When I looked it up it said that I must be clear to the angels about what I want. I started a manifestation course with

Protected Awakenings

Gabby Bernstein for 21 days, so I started writing down what I wanted to manifest for my life. I used to think numerology was a whole other language and now I see it is. Be open to the numbers and guidance waiting all around that will prove you are always protected.

Protected Lesson - Step 2
Let go and Let God

When you see angel numbers, let go and let God. This was a saying that my friend Eugenia used to say. See the numbers and know their presence. If they are letting you know they are there, be happy that you are supported in what you are doing right now. Give over what you can't handle, acknowledge that they are standing by your side. Remember angels can be in groups and they will surround you, sometimes 10,000 of them. Make a note of the time and speak to them. They want you to be aware of them.

I once spoke to a girl on Instagram who helped me understand numbers even more. I told her how I made an alarm in my phone that appeared at **11:11** so I would always see the numbers and that I use Gabby Bernstein's mantra.

> *"Everything is happening around me and I am truly cared for."*—*Gabby Bernstein*

I was told not to chase the numbers, now I realise you don't need to chase the angels who always guide you, they are there to remind you that you're not alone and any time you think you are, think again. That day I took off the angel alarm and let go and let God.

Angel Numbers

The next day I noticed that Gabby Bernstein was live on Instagram, and I said "thank you that I am on her live podcast called Dear Gabby" before she started choosing people, I journaled **"thank you that I am speaking to Gabby"** and shut my journal and thought about something else. **I let go,** I picked up my journal, put my phone down and turned my thoughts to writing about my day. My phone lit up; **Gabby wants to go live with you!**

I couldn't believe it; I was talking to Gabby Bernstein herself. I had let go, I didn't obsess about how I had to talk to her or that nothing good happens to me like I usually did, I thanked God, and a real angel came to see me.

You can do this too and you can always let go. Tell God or the Universe what you really want and don't overthink it have faith that you will get it and move on.

Protected Lesson - Step 3
Say thank you for guiding me

Think about all the angels who are working hard for you, and no one thanks them. They save lives, stop tragedies, intervene in situations we know nothing about and still we just expect everything to work out. Grab your journal and write a thank you letter, or write a thank you now here in this book.

Thank you, angels,

For always guiding me, watching over me, lighting up a path to the place you know I should be, protected by you now and always.

Protected Awakenings

Notice how you feel after this prayer and after writing it down, go about your day or write this down first thing tomorrow morning.

By reading this book you know of all the ways you have been protected, loved, guided, raised, seen and heard. I pray that you always realise, feel and make notes of this presence that's always available to you, awaiting you and watching you while you breathe into the life that is the light in your body that you share with yourself and your guardian angels now and forever.

So share this knowledge with your loved ones that God is forever there no matter what, awaken those who live in fear and remind them the universe is always listening and waiting for your reply.

CHAPTER 12
The angel I never saw coming

I never had anyone listen to me like her, someone who didn't judge me. Someone who didn't intimidate me, she understood me, wanted to help me and wanted to see what more she could do.

I can't believe I spoke to her for that long, that she really wanted to understand my point of view. In the process I never thought she would become a close friend. I was reading **The Science Of Getting Rich by Wallace Wattles,** studying it and highlighting every page.

While I completely became myself and told her the story of a book I was reading and learning about and how I had a dream about it, that I should read it, highlight every page and make notes all over the book, I never thought it would change my life and the way I saw the world.

She was understanding, kind and had that instinctive feeling to help me even if I didn't ask.

Protected Awakenings

She anticipated what I needed, and I was so grateful to have her in my presence.

People who do the same thing day in and day out, don't know how amazing they are, they don't see how beneficial they are to the outside world.

For someone to be so outspoken and so open with me, I was completely and honestly shocked for someone to become so close to me.

In that short time, I knew her, she helped me more than ever and completely channelled how I felt to the point that I felt better only when she was around.

Her aura and energy calmed me. She was the only one who understood me.

I met a lot of nurses, and she was a nurse with the heart and aura I needed to focus on my healing.

There are only a few of these people around and they will help put you back into your heart as you stress about being in your mind.

Some people are lucky enough to encounter a nurse like her and others only see them for five minutes.

I wrote thank you cards, I wanted to acknowledge those who helped me, changed my mind and encouraged me to keep going.

The people in your life that hold your head up, give you wisdom and make you think or make you stop and help you to do more with your life.

The angel I never saw coming

For all those people are angels, you may have needed another perspective on your life, another way out and another heart that heard yours and another person that sees the light in you.

For all the angels are here to hear your heart, to find out what is weighing you down and take away the heaviness on your shoulders.

Every angel wants to spread light not just metaphorically but also literally and wants you to find your own light to spread to others.

For Pooja was only one of the angels I met, and it did not stop there, but I felt honoured to have met her and have her to remind me that I am not alone and I'm never too far from another angel I have not met yet.

Pooja listened to me talk when I was high from painkillers talking about the law of attraction and how the world should be and as I spoke for hours I noticed she stayed in the room and listened and only because of her I would look forward to her coming to check up on me and actually asking how I was and not just checking my blood pressure and acting like all the other nurses who subconsciously act like robots every day. While Covid was still happening and I had no family around me I was even more grateful for Pooja for telling me how strong I am, reminding me that in the end it will be ok and talking about God and praying for those who are in need right now.

When we wake up in the morning, we turn on the news and listen to all the negative stories in the world, even if we

Protected Awakenings

don't watch the news there is that post that says sensitive content that is going viral that everyone asks you if you've seen. We think that it's the end of the world because we want all the friends that we have on Facebook and Instagram to be there at our party. All these beliefs that we have somehow created that society told us seem to add up. In my story I thought that every nurse and doctor would help me straight away when in my case all I needed was Pooja to be there to remind me I was heard and seen.

I shouted at many doctors and had a go at many physio therapists, I fought and really had an ugly side of my ego that I didn't like. I did all of this out of fear, even though I gave thank you cards to everyone, deep down I felt so guilty even now that I am writing a book about light, love, angels and being protected when I acted as though I had none. After some of my biggest awakenings.

Pooja really was there for me, and she was the ONLY one I needed and that has happened all my life. I had one amazing friend while everyone else bullied me. I had one activity as a child I loved that I liked more than all the others.

So, whatever or whoever that person is in your life, appreciate them today. God gave you them to get through your life today. They are your protection and light, tell them today how much they mean to you, whoever they are.

In these three steps I want you to think of all those people who were put there to intervene in your life to bring you back to your heart.

The angel I never saw coming

Protected Lesson - Step 1
Ask the angels to put you back in your heart

Sometimes we overthink far too much, and we get in our own way. When I met Pooja, I was so angry, relying on my own strength and always thinking that everything had to be a certain way. When we think that we are not listened to and that nothing good happens to us, we tell God or the Universe that we are not grateful for what we have. We start to block the help that the angels want to guide us with. Ask the angels to get you back into your heart and do this by distancing yourself from the frantic mind.

Say the prayer with me.

Stay with me during this difficult time, send me guidance and put my heart back in place, let my heartbeat to calm me down. Let my mind have peace and let my heart share love and light, let me see the peace that was always within me.

I hope you feel better from saying this prayer, I hope you remember it whenever you feel your mind wonder off into angry land, don't stay there it's not you. Tell the angels to help you and guide you back to your true self. Surrender and ask for more help in the situation you're dealing with.

Protected Lesson - Step 2
Pray that the light returns to them

When I sent Pooja the card, I only realised afterwards that I really prayed the light would return to her. Being an empath,

Protected Awakenings

I can feel the energy of others, positive or negative. I know if someone is burnt out, tired, exhausted or just overworked and barely getting by. When I wrote that card, I didn't think, I just started to free write, and the words came out of me. I wanted to share the light she shared with me. The smiles she gave me, I wanted her to smile too. She saw me well and out of hospital, she didn't treat me like all the other patients, she treated me like a human who had more to give and more to love. You too have way more to give your angels, you may have a friend that you vent to all the time, why don't you send them a present for no reason. Pray that the person receives the light they gave to you and pray that they get that light repeatedly for everyone is fighting a hard battle.

Repeat this and write down what you want for them

If someone makes you happy, make them happier.
—Unknown

God/Universe, send light to those who give it away so easily. For the ones who cared to listen and the one who makes my life better. Hold them and cloak them with an energy and a ring of light now and forever, give them an angel unexpectedly forever.

Protected Lesson - Step 3
Describe to them how much they helped you

The people who help us the most need to hear how much they mean to you. Sometimes I think about how regret is worse than anything else. I regret not going to see my granny enough even though she is my guardian angel now and I can

The angel I never saw coming

talk to her anytime. I miss talking to her about everything. Make sure you tell those in your life that you appreciate them, you are so thankful for them and explain in detail the obvious. When you do this, you are acknowledging who is a true earth angel in your life. If you look around properly you will find them all around, you. If you stay stagnant in the world you won't see them at all and if you've had many awakenings, you will see nothing but angels. Tell them thank you, explain how much they helped you in depth. The depth to your thankfulness will not go unnoticed.

Some people come to your rescue so quickly and you must be thankful. In my story I really had to get out of my ego and see the angel I had in front of me listening and cheering me on. I thanked her so much and I want you to see the people who really made a difference and give them a random act of kindness today, show them they are seen and heard. Talking about thankfulness I want to tell you in the next chapter about my friend who changed my mindset even more by telling me about gratitude and how much it can help you manifest all your desires and change your life.

CHAPTER 13
Gratitude Angel

Another amazing human I want to call an earth angel is Danijela Jukic who lives in Ohio in the US. I never knew the impact she would have now on so many of us in such an important time of our lives to understand the meaning of gratitude and the power it has to improve your life. Danijela found the book **The Magic - by Rhonda Byrne** and started a zoom call sharing a chapter a day of the book so that we could practise a 28-day challenge.

The book includes Rhonda Byrne's life and practising being grateful for every area, mistake, blessing and moment that got you to where you are now. Doing this daily over nineteen months she encouraged us all to practise as much as we can. Without realising we very ungrateful in life, as we complain we attract what we don't want into our lives. I hear people say all the time write down three things that you are grateful for, but I feel that this is not enough. Rhonda Byrne says every day write down ten things you are grateful for and explain in detail, where I pour my heart out with my true thankfulness for my life of how I'm feeling and connect to my God with what's in my heart in all my written blessings. If it wasn't for all the gratitude and feelings I had written down, I really believe I wouldn't have had the positive mindset I have or even be alive today without Danijela.

Every day she would get on zoom, no matter how she was feeling, to talk about what she sees in the chapter we had for that day. Writing in a journal really showed me how lucky I was to have all I have in my life. From the smallest things to the big things, I hold in my heart I was amazed every day by how much had flowed out of me that I had unlocked and heard about in others. A month ago, I was also part of a book called 'Heartset' and when I let my friend read my part of the book, she said she can hear how grateful I truly am for life, which made me so emotional. Gratitude has opened my heart and made me see that family are a blessing and if you're not grateful for what you have it will be taken away from you which scares me more than anything else in the world. I have witnessed Danijela and all of us on the gratitude call see the **depth of gratitude** which attracts **more positivity** and **more blessings** to you immediately.

I have never said this too Danijela and she will read this for herself, but she has changed the lives of so many, been an angel to us all and even to the people pouring gratitude into their friends and family putting them on another vibration and frequency that changes the world. For Danijela to be so vulnerable and sharing her understanding of gratitude and what it means to be in love with all your life. I believe that thankfulness is the key to everything when God sees that you

Gratitude Angel

are thankful for what he has given you, he will bless you even more.

God is always giving and whatever you do, whether you practise gratitude or not, the universe is always giving, to activate more blessings to you. If you want to be more grateful start here.

When your key goes through the front door say thank you, when a friend is there for you when no one else is, say thank you and think about how many angels you are thanking right now.

Some days, honestly, I don't sit in gratitude as much as other days. I don't feel like doing my gratitude and that is the day I need to write gratitude even more.

I used to have a very chaotic life and even though I let anxiety grab hold of me more than faith. I was ungrateful, I lost myself, I had lost my real heart and my true self.

When I'm in gratitude I am back in my heart. I'm thankful for the real treasure in my life. When I'm in my heart I look at everything with love, I get to see the sunset because I am alive. I am lucky enough to breathe in fresh air when there are others in hospital now, wishing and praying to be outside in nature. There is someone right now praying for the job you can't stand. The power of two words can really wake you up to see the life you are living is someone else's dream.

When someone thanks me, for example when I teach swimming and a parent tells their child to say thank you, I now feel completely different like God/the universe is really

Protected Awakenings

saying thank you to me for just existing and you can feel that too. When you get a coffee and someone hands you anything look in their eyes and feel them smile at you, feel them connect to that split second, that's God through them saying thank you.

Now I can feel when someone is ungrateful for someone or a situation, they lose interest and the gratitude fades from everything. Don't let that happen to you, that is not life.

I'm thankful for my grandparents on both sides of my family and for all their prayers. I'm thankful for all the love I have had in my life because the love that my parents showed me, I have given to others, whether they accepted it or not, I am grateful. It's not always how they accept but how you give from a good heart. I gave to others to the point where I have had people say, wow, you really care a lot, don't you? I take this as a compliment, and I pray I always do. Why did I give so much? Because that's all I knew and saw growing up, gratitude is love and love is all you are and all you should be to yourself and all those who are desperately searching for it.

I believe that if we are not sitting in gratitude then we are sitting in lack and if we are sitting in lack then we are not living at all.

You don't have to believe in what I believe in, but I want you to know that the more you are thankful for the invisible realm of angels that support you and protect you, you will be aware of the love that is spirituality that will capture your heart and protect you forever if you simply say thank you.

Gratitude Angel

Giving God/your angels your gratitude and heart is an act of thanking your ancestors for pushing you through to where you are today.

If we are not in gratitude, we are in lack were the enemy wants us to think we have nothing left, this is not true. It costs nothing to say thank you, but it costs everything in the world if you only look at the lack. If you walk around saying I lack this and I lack that you will feel low, and attract a low vibe frequency, the universe picks up on this and then you attract more of what you don't want.

The law of attraction picks up your frequency.

When I first started learning about the law of attraction, I found this concept hard to grasp, however, after reading about it more, I now see why Einstein said thank you hundreds of times a day.

"He thanked all the great scientists who had preceded him for their contribution which had enabled him to learn and achieve even more in his work and eventually become one of the greatest scientists who has ever lived." – The Secret

Think about yourself in the same way. Be thankful for your grandparents who taught your parents all they knew and taught you what you know now.

Living in lack is a bad habit, a bad habit that you didn't mean to pick up, but it doesn't have to be this way. Every day is a fresh start and everyday there is something to be thankful for. Once you see that, every miracle in your life will become more and more magical as you go on.

Protected Awakenings

Follow Danijela on Instagram **@danijelajukic1** Message her to be part of the life of gratitude group chat and community of people all around the world that have manifested miracles.

When I practised my gratitude, I once wrote a letter to my granny. I thanked her for how she told me to always say thank you and talked to her about my love of dancing. Which made me want to dance more and chase my dreams. I thanked her for listening to me and for inspiring me to be my true self and to be confident and stand up for what I believe in and be the girl I always was in my heart.

As I wrote this letter my brother was texting me at the same time and I noticed the sun beaming down on me through the window. My brother was talking about how Olga was a part of his presentation at work, and I slowly started to cry as I was sensing her and how she was with me. As I started reading his text I burst into tears as the sun was on my shoulders. As the tears flowed, I thanked her, and she was in two places at the same time. I cried tears of joy and the feeling of love moved through my body for I know she was there, and she knew every word I had written. I knew my guardian angel was there, listening.

Protected Lesson - Step 1
Write a gratitude letter to your guardian angels

You may never have done anything like this, or you may know someone close to you that passed, and you feel they are protecting you. Say thank you for all their prayers and how they protect you in this realm and another.

Gratitude Angel

Write down this prayer.......

To my guardian angel_____*Write their name* _____

Thank you for showing me the way...

Thank you for your invisible golden light, I feel you now as I reach to you, you taught me _____ *fill in the blank*

_____

_____ **You know if I had another chance to speak to you now, this is what I would say.**

If you too want to feel their presence, pray for this in your own time and say this prayer whenever you feel like it and come back to it and sit in thankfulness for their voice, there time and all the moments you were with them.

Thank them for everything, for example, I thank my granny for the songs she used to sing to me when I was a baby, and all the cuddles she used to give me and every time she listened to me complain then and now. Say thank you here and write down everything about them now.

Thank you for _____

_____

_____

_____

_____

Protected Lesson - Step 2
Feel the angels' positive energy

If you want more positive energy, practise gratitude. Being grateful is stepping into the peace that is available to you. I have learnt that slowly, but I want you to learn my shortcuts to a more positive life. I am still practising; as well as our guardian angels who protect us, we also have guiding angels who walk with us as we grow, evolve and develop our understanding of our journey.

Practise your positive energy and journal your new perspective with these angels and be grateful for the good, the bad and the ugly as it makes you stronger. It is who you are and it's all lessons from God or the universe.

Write down here what makes you positive and on a high vibrational frequency. Do more of these things and think about what makes you feel good so that you can be with your angels to thank them. It could be music or working out. Write down what makes you feel good here for good feelings are what you want more of.

I feel good when I _____

_____
_____
_____
_____
_____
_____

Gratitude Angel

Say this out loud afterwards

Thank you, angels, for always giving me great energy, lots of love and good feelings., angels remind me of what I love to do, guide me to my true heart and great feelings always. Thank you here and now.

Protected Lesson - Step 3
Be thankful for your life so far

To have more magic, more angels and more love in your life, be grateful for all you have and all you have seen so far. I'm grateful for my ex-boyfriend for loving me when he loved me the most, when he helped me the most through a really hard time in my life.

I'm grateful for everything I manifested and my whole life.I flew to the Maldives, got the job I wanted, and I was in love. I couldn't have asked for more, but most importantly I recognised that none of it would have been possible if I wasn't thankful for the life God gave me. The burning desire I have that leads me to want to know more about Him and to help awaken you to the truth of angels and that you are protected like the spiritual experiences I have shared in this book and that we are all here for more reasons than you and I will ever know.

So be thankful for your whole life. I'm thankful for all my hardships because they made me write this book for you.

So, write with me now and write down the parts of your life you're grateful for with all your heart. It could be when

Protected Awakenings

you got married or when you had a child. Say thank you for all the moments you wish you could bring back, bring them back now, let your soul go there and come back in this room. As your soul moves all the time. Let's go there now in your life and write down three moments you loved with all your heart.

_____

_____

_____

Now say thank you for all the amazing new moments you will have that you're being guided to with your guardian angels and so that you can live the amazing magical life that you really dream of. Your angels want you to live there too. There is more abundance waiting for you and more love that will ignite you.

_____

_____

_____

    Be thankful for the little things and the big things and thank all your angels that you have seen and had some of the most amazing times and experiences in your life. Hold on to that and believe that there is more. For the more thankful you are, the more you are saying thank you for the future and the life you haven't even lived yet. Be thankful for your future self.

Gratitude Angel

To practise more of this, watch this video of Tony Robbins

https://www.youtube.com/watch?v=faTGTgid8Uc&t=5s

In this chapter I want you to know the importance of gratitude. If you want to, you can read the book 'The Magic' by Rhonda Byrne. Join us on the Danijela's zoom call every day at 11am EST 'The life of gratitude'. In the three steps above write a letter to your guardian angels to say thank you. Remember that you also have guiding angels guiding you to what is best for you and if you want to sit in this space more, you can have a look at Tony Robbins' priming video on the link above to sit in gratitude and breathe in the present moment given to you here and now. Start where you are.

In the next chapter I will tell you a story about how someone had forgotten the angels and how you should never forget the support around you. Walk with me as this story touched my heart, I hope it holds yours too in the awareness I had.

CHAPTER 14
Don't forget the angels

I was leaving my favourite coffee shop thinking I had come to the end of this book only to realise there was more, more to tell you, more that God had placed on my heart and more to awaken you to. As I left, I bumped into my friend Jolanta, who I told you about in chapter 5. While we were chatting about spirituality and life, I caught her say *"I don't worry about my children as the angels look after them"*. Hearing this I asked her how she knew about the angels and when she had become aware of them. Jolanta smiled and said it was a great story and I knew I was about to hear something I had to tell you. Jolanta explained that she had bought a small gift of a little angel with a gemstone on it. She got the gift from a shop that was selling crystals and she really thought it would make a nice present for someone but at the time she wasn't sure who. At that time her mother was in hospital and her sister went to see her and Jolanta said she would go later. That day she decided to give the angel gift to her mother and her mother quizzed her. Jolanta explained to her mother that when she was a child,

Protected Awakenings

she used to tell her about all the angels -what they did, who they were, and their importance in the world. "So, I got you this gift to remind you of what you used to tell me." Angel Michael is also the angel of healing and when you talk to him it is believed that if you tell him what's wrong and ask for help, he will heal you and take away your pain and suffering. I have heard this before of people meditating on Archangel Michael and healing faster. I was stunned by what I saw next. I looked outside the window and a light caught my attention. While Jolanta was talking about angels, I saw a guy getting on his motor bike. He turned the lights on before he drove off and the lights were the exact shape of angel wings. I had to interrupt Jolanta to show her as she was telling me this story, they glowed at me like a sign to say we are real, and we are always around you and a thank you for telling the world. I felt excited, overjoyed and determined to carry on with this book, excited to think that we are not alone but looked after. This protection can follow you wherever you go; all you must do is believe in them and speak to them.

I know this was another sign and another confirmation that they are always around us. I still have goosebumps thinking that she told me this while I saw that they were listening. As soon as I saw this, I wanted to share it with you.

If you have ever experienced an angel, awoken to their presence, seen them in a dream or know they are watching over you, don't forget them, remember them always, know they are by your side watching the world with you. They are

Don't forget the angels

cheering you on and they are always looking for your heart, to heal you, guide you, and pick up from where they left off, where you have fallen. **Never forget the angels** and never forget your true heart.

When great things happen to us, we think that was only then. It won't happen again. We think this is where we are now and that we can never change, that is a lie. When I prayed to Archangels Michael and Raphael, they took all pain away from me, I don't even remember what it was like. I really believe that we can hand anything over and sit in a real place of change if we remember they are there and they hold us. As I surrender my life to God every day and make this a daily habit, I won't ever forget the people, angels and beings who are put there to intervene in the helping and healing we need all the time. So, talk to them, remember them in your hardest times, your brightest days, and that their constant support is always there.

The enemy wants you to forget this and to think you are alone. That it's the end and that your life doesn't change, and this is exactly how he takes so many souls. Angels want you to wake up and be awakened that you are never alone. When Jesus spoke to Jolanta after her car accident and told her to go back to earth, he awakened her when she thought her life was over. The angels do the same, they hold you and see how precious your life is no matter what you went through because you are not the situation, you are not what happened to you, you are always your creator's child. **Never forget this support and knowing,** I say this for me too. I speak to God like my best friend, and I love that I can talk to him anywhere and at any time of the day. For I won't forget when he came to me and if I do ever forget then I feel lost and I'm not where I am meant to be.

So, I want you to remember this guidance, I want you to remember this time and take it with you wherever you go so that if you too ever need healing, you know how, when and where to go. **Ask Archangel Michael and Archangel Raphael** to hold you and heal you now and always and God or the Universe will bring them to you.

Protected Lesson Step 1
Jolanta protects her mum

Jolanta didn't forget the angels and she reminded her mum of all that she had taught her. Jolanta protected her by wishing the best for her and not trying to take all the responsibility of healing her by giving her a gift.

Who would you give this book to while they are in need?

What gifts can you give to let people know you are there for them?

I have gifted people devotionals, cards, books and recommended prayers and affirmations where I thought God was telling me to do that for them. We are never alone in this world.

Imagine for one moment that prayer protected your whole life.

Don't forget the angels

Send a gift, let someone know you care, tell someone you will pray for them, send them words of affirmation, say what I want for you is eg. love, light, healing, a brighter future etc. List idea's here, happiness, peace, clarity. _____

_____

_____

_____

_____

For this is a form of prayer, every word you say is a prayer that you want to tell someone, tell the universe today, you are heard, valued and listened to by an angel.

I don't know who needs to hear this. I silenced my voice for a long time, told myself I was not heard and invaluable to the world. I held my heart so close, I felt it was hard to breathe. I told myself no one cares, when people care so much you get tired of people asking how you are. I held my own hand when no one was watching. I looked in the mirror into the iris of my own eye and someone said (God). You are seen and you are heard. The one that will look after you is you, and my free writing will be heard.

Protected Lesson Step 2
Make sure you lead with love

Sometimes people don't want to receive gifts, lead with love anyway. Sometimes people are confused that you gave them something and think they need to give you something, lead with love anyway. For if people can hate for no reason, you can love for no reason and give for no reason.

Protected Awakenings

If you want, you can read about the law of giving and receiving and you will see why this is so important. For I feel the same about angels, they love you no matter how stubborn your heart is, they love you even if you haven't surrendered your everything. But whatever you do, lead with love and love all they are and just remind them they are not alone in how they feel. For if they have you, this book and a whole team of angels I have opened you to or added to your knowledge of angels and they are all behind you all the way and I pray they brighten up your day,

So, lead with love even if you don't always feel it around you.

Protected Lesson Step 3
How to remember the angels

Remembering all the angels and support around me is a daily practice. Every morning I write my gratitude and I say thank you for my God, my family and all the family that is no longer with me and those who have turned into angels. I pray, I read my devotional and I do some angel meditations at night. These meditations are my favourite. I look up Archangel Michael prayers, articles and posts and give over what I cannot handle.

The world can drag you down and angels lift you up. Be the hope you were looking for in others. Flick a page in the bible and see if there is a message for you today. You can connect to angels anytime, talk to them like they are with you in person. You can ask to see them in a dream, ask God to show you an angel for a sign or speak to them knowing

Don't forget the angels

they are watching you and remember that they are guiding you, loving you and waiting for you to pick up more love and light all the time.

Don't forget the angels and what you have learnt from my lessons. Give a prayer, a gift, be there for a friend, give over what you want for them. Lead with love and read about the law of giving and receiving. Remember the support available to you and give light and love in the world. In the next chapter I will show you how to ask for a surprise from your angels and how you can do this whenever you want.

CHAPTER 15

Ask the angels to surprise you

Angels are a lot of fun and I want you to know this for yourself, don't just take my word for it. I want you to ask to see how they give you more love in your day.

I saw a post that said

"The angels are delivering you a beautiful surprise today. Your angel is here to help you, whether it be a parking spot, an unexpected conversation, a loving moment. Ask them for surprises and they will be delivered.

@ellaringrose

When I saw this this post I smiled asking for a surprise for the day. That morning I did my gratitude and sent it to my friend Gigi who is another friend I met through Sean G Murphy.

When I sent my blessings you could hear Sean in the background of the video telling a story of how he saw a

Protected Awakenings

picture of his wife with the words *call her on* the picture. Hearing this Gigi thought this was a sign that the universe was telling her to call me.

Gigi messaged me saying she thought the universe was telling her to call me. I looked at this message and smiled thinking that was the surprise. The angels directed Gigi to call me from Florida but then I realised that that was not the only surprise, another story I felt to share for you here.

I really thought I had finished with all my awakenings and all my stories of the supernatural and surprises. I had heard about the protected angelic support between these pages, but I was not prepared for the story Gigi was about to tell me. Gigi asked how I was, and I asked her also. I updated her on how I met Jolanta and how I felt I had a responsibility to awaken the world to what I am learning. I explained what my writing was about and how it was about spirituality. I had not explained in lots of detail that it was about angels yet.

Telling her about my book, I was so nervous as everyone's response is different, but as I explained to her, she listened even more because she to has a love and understanding of how powerful spirituality can be. As Gigi opened up to me in our conversation, she told me that she had seen a spirit and that she had felt an overwhelming sense of love that she would do anything to feel again. I told Gigi to message me everything she saw so I could make this my last chapter for you as angels and spirits come in all forms and they are more real than ever.

Ask the angels to surprise you

The message below was written by Gigi and I wanted to keep it exactly the way she told it.

In the summer of 2019, it was August I believe, and I had just started meditating and I started to get addicted to the feeling I would get before, during and after my meditations. I used to wake up real early on the days I worked in the afternoon to watch the sunrise. Living in southwest Florida the weather is beautiful all year round. One morning as I looked out, I did my usual routine. I came outside and there was still some of the morning fog clearing the sun was peeking through the trees. As the nocturnal animals changed shifts with the crepuscular animals the sun started to rise. I took my position on my yoga mat sat cross legged and began my ritual of setting the mood, and as I looked, I saw a figure, yet it wasn't like a figure it was more like a blob. You know when it's hot outside and you can see the heat rising off the ground, there were waves suspended in mid-air about three feet off the ground. I stared at it in amazement coupled with confusion and a little bit of wonder.

Asking myself what is that? What is that? ... and then after what felt like eternity it vanished. I sat there in awe and confusion. I really thought I was hallucinating or going crazy. At that moment I thought I had lost all my marbles. It wasn't until later that day when I told my father, who is a very spiritual man, the story of my experience. that he nonchalantly said to me "Oh, that's a spirit". That was the first of my many spiritual experiences, and it wasn't until now, this moment of

Protected Awakenings

me writing this, that I am aware of every second we should be open, receptive and present.

—Gina.E.Francois

I too have had spiritual experiences that are hard to explain but I wanted to tell you this story because a friend also sent me a video of a helicopter lifting off the ground and as the person inside passes away a white spirit shoots out of the top of a helicopter. This can only be seen on the video because the video was recorded at night and I have watched it a hundred times. I was in awe. When I showed my friend Jolanta she told me to notice the white spirit turned from a light bulb shape like a blob just like Gigi saw into a bright figure. The white light then shoots out shoots so fast like a line you see in the clouds that an aeroplane has made but this was in the night sky. There are many spirit guides and white lights around us we do not see and as Gigi said we must be open to it, receive it and accept it and not walk around blinded by the supernatural. I have spoken to God as though I don't believe he is there for me and then ever so suddenly felt him wrap around me like a blanket covering my whole body with a cloak of love like he really came to hug me and said you don't need anyone else when you have me. I went straight to sleep.

So, open up to good angels and let them guide you and be open to them, they want to show you they are here and there is a whole unseen world that connects to yours. I have spoken to my father about things I have seen in my meditations. He told me now and again he smells his grandmother around him, and I was reading about that only a few days before he

Ask the angels to surprise you

told me, spirits are definitely around us and we should be aware of them.

So, as I asked for a surprise, and I heard this story. **So, what will your angels surprise you with today? Will it be a phone call from a friend? Will it be a great idea? Will it be a white feather falling on the grass a sign or something you have been waiting for?**

For me sometimes it's messaging someone. You never know, so ask today and just ask angels; **how will you surprise me today?**

We live in such a strange world where angels, spirits, God and the Universe are all real. I used to think that some things were made up and others had these stories just to scare us. We live in such a big unexplained world that we choose what we believe in and that everything else is a hallucination or it wasn't real. When I started reading Gabrielle Bernstein's book super attractor, she had a chapter that talked about seeing white light. The more I was reading the more I started seeing it too. Seeing this glowing white light everywhere I too thought I was hallucinating thinking maybe I should stop reading this book. All these experiences are real and the more you practise these things you will start to feel more protected, listened to and loved by another presence. We don't believe that angels will surprise us, we are too busy walking around asleep to the realm all around us. We don't ask God or the Universe to surprise us because we don't believe that it will happen but when you do this for yourself you will see how your day connects because you asked for it

Protected Awakenings

to happen. Ask for your life to be beautiful and watch it all unfold before you.

In the next three steps I want you to ask, and I will teach you how to ask your angels to surprise you. Do this for yourself and I would love to know what happens. Message me on Instagram @yessicaxjessica and tell me all that happens to you.

Protected Lesson - Step 1
Ask

Look in the mirror, smile and ask the angels: How will you surprise me today? Then walk away, read a book, look at your phone, and do something different. Your angels are always guiding you, awakening you and wanting you to be in your higher self, not your subconscious self-doing the same thing every day. They want you to feel good, loved, valued and surprised. Claim your surprise and then move on with your day.

Protected Lesson - Step 2
Let go

Let go of what you think the surprise might be, let go of expectation, I thought Gigi was just calling me to check up on me, I didn't think she would be in my book also. I got two surprises in one, but we all find this, sometimes we get more than we asked for when we step out of our own way. God or the universe has so many surprises and blessings in store for us.

Ask the angels to surprise you

Protected Lesson - Step 3
Write down your surprises

Journal your surprises and make sure you write the date and time. How long did it take till you got a surprise? The best part of learning is in the duplication, when you learn a skill and do it again and again. When you get a surprise and then you can surprise others randomly, you know that angels support you and you support angels. Journal how you learn to connect with angels and what they give you and how you are aware of this journey because its personal to you. For the more protection you feel, the more you can pass that on to your friends and family when they need it most.

So, journal every surprise, every encounter and every unexpected moment where you know you are being guided. You may have several surprises in one day. Write them all down and be grateful for all you were given in the day.

Angels are fun and they love to surprise you and everyone. I feel that this story had to go in this book because I got two surprises in one to awaken you to the spirit, how real they are and to give you another chance to feel heard. You are awakened by the guidance of your heart and the synchronicities given to you by angelic support that surrounds you and guides you every day even in this moment right now.

You may call it God/Universe/Angels or even spirit, depending on the higher power that you believe in, talk to them often and know they love you, guide you and want you to be more than you ever imagined for yourself.

Protected Awakenings

For I pray you feel this, wake with this thought in mind and fall into this knowing and longing for your heart to stay in its true self.

Ask for surprises, journal your own journey of spirituality and what it means to you.

As I end this book, I have no more practices for you I just want to say thank you, thank you for reading this far, thank you for being open to every title and every topic I have discussed and every angel I have introduced you to. For I hope that you feel a presence bigger than you, I pray you feel love that you cannot explain, I pray you find gratitude in all you do and all you see in your world. I pray angels hold you here.

If you want to know more, keep reading, keep connecting, keep meditating and praying for your breakthroughs. They will happen in perfect timing, and I pray that God/the universe and all the angels show you heaven on earth and protect you now and forever in their name. For every angel with us now and every angel you need will protect you and be with you wherever you go. For when the invisible realm is not invisible anymore your awareness will become an awakening you can never ignore.

For the protection I had in my darkest days is here for you also. I pray that whatever you are going through or have been through, that it all turns into peace. For that peace will fulfil you, ignite you and help you to walk in the light of today. For you are always looked after, please give this book to someone who really needs it or leave it on a bus, leave it

Ask the angels to surprise you

on the train, write your name and phone number in the front of it and wonder where it will go. Buy this book and leave it on a wall or a park bench, for we all need protection, and we all need to believe in something and that someone is holding us with every step. I will step with you towards that beaming light that your angel wants to show you. This book is yours please write all over it, your prayers and findings, pray with it and read it over and over for what you learn is yours and how you interrupt my words is all yours and let light lead your life and your way and you will forever be guided. Thank you for hearing my awakenings and taking this journey with me for this book would never have happened if I had stayed asleep in the world that dims our light. Thank you for reading my words taking my steps to connect and to stay in the message that was given to me to channel my writing and fall on the page, that you and I are forever protected wherever we go, thank you for awakening and thank you for adding to the light of the world.

Lead with Love and Light and tell your angels where you need them the most. For I pray you find peace, love and more blessings and that you too encounter your own spiritual experiences that you know someone was there and someone was watching you, for with God I pray that your life only gets better and better and you manifest more than you ever imagined your life to be with love.

Live the most beautiful life, live knowing a million angels protect you forever, lots of love – *Jessica*

About the Author

Jessica Is a swimming teacher from North-West London. She has taught all age groups in Spain and Greece in all-inclusive hotels as well as dancing, singing and helping all the guests on holiday. As well as working abroad she has travelled a lot with her family while manifesting anything she wanted. After a horrible incurable cancer diagnosis plus reading about spirituality during lockdown, she realised she had a gift for writing to heal herself and others. Jessica's freewriting surprises her as she is channelled by a higher power. Jessica thinks more people need to have awakenings to experience freedom and the true love of life that has always been within them they just forgot it was there.

To follow her on Instagram, go to **@yessicaxjessica**

Afterword

In January 2021, I remember writing in a journal, thank you, thank you, thank you that I am cancer free, but the day I was in remission came even faster. From doctors saying I may have five years left of life to others telling me this is the end of the road, I kept my faith, I used to fear death and be constantly anxious and have faced depression many times only to find that it was never the end. The positive Jessica I am today had a complete rebirth and came back almost where I think I had a past life and I felt like someone else, I miss the girl I was and I dream about her everyday only to realise I am still capable of having her all back, full of energy full of life and more miracles and manifestations than anyone imagined. From breaking my back in three places and learning to walk again, being told I'm too young to have cancer, shaving my head and embracing it, to going back to work sensing there is more to life than all this. I was inspired by Gabby Bernstein and have been lucky enough to speak to her on Instagram and online events, following her teachings and having a mentor I really believe that God prepared me before I faced the valley of death or at the least the valley, I thought I was in this awakening was only the beginning. A new beginning to healing, helping myself, healing myself and inspiring others to do the same.

Protected Awakenings

I decided I wanted to write a book and did a course with Gabby Bernstein which had meditations to follow. One of the meditations lead me to free writing when asked the questions what is the book that the world needs now? this is what I had written.......

Protected.......

Guidance synchronicities and angelic support.

Love, Joy and guidance in the sea of God moving in and out to completely let go of what was. Breathe into what is beginning and what's ending. Be guided in the knowing that everything will be alright. We are all protected in a circle in this vortex of love that we call life. We see love, we feel love, we want love, and we are love. When we are protected, we can see all the light and love around us when we depart from anxiety and despair, we lose sight of what's important who needs us and how a higher power is following us and constantly moving towards the next step to heal us and guide us to the love that was always there and available to us always. He is called God.

After this one session I had no idea what it all meant but I knew my message was important. I spoke to my brother about a title for my book and I thought of the idea *Protected Awakenings* and he asked me who are they protected by? To which I thought well by God. As God knew I would be saved and I would stay alive.

Afterword

After making a fifteen second reel on Instagram of my whole cancer journey, I found strength in my vulnerability. I found healing and learnt more about psychology and energy. I saw my inner child and have had experiences people pay for, from learning how to acknowledge her and hold her when she's crying, I felt a shift in the way I see inner peace. I learnt about being an empath and that I was always absorbing other energies all my life and felt into a place where I was manifesting all the wrong energy however life does not have to be like that, we are all here for a reason and it's up to us to keep finding out what that is. What's our burning desire? What does our heartbeat for? Who does our heartbeat for? And at the end of it all who will you thank when your world turns into more magic than you planned.

For I hope you find encouragement in my writing, love and wonder. I want you to have questions, start conversations and be open to the idea that what if you were always protected and you really felt that. Before you go to sleep, I would like you to ask your angels to appear in your dreams to speak to you and please let me know what happens. Because before I finished editing this manuscript I went and bought a pandora bracelet and the woman helping me said I could get a bracelet for free, so I had a look and I couldn't decide on a charm for it as I have so many at home, telling her this she said to me that if I couldn't decide I could get the angel charm and I glanced with a smile, after writing this book I told her it's funny you say that because I do believe in angels while I remember looking out the shop window at a girl with shoulder length curly hair wearing all white, a white top, white jogging bottoms, white trainers and

Protected Awakenings

what felt like me seeing in slow motion this girl talking to her friend walking by, (this is my sign that life is going in the right direction) cutting short my awakening of my sign the assistant in the shop said **oh so do I, I believe in angels and my whole bracelet I have on is for my dad.** At that point I felt drawn to her instantly and I feel drawn to you, to remind you to be the light, be an angel for someone else, ask any angel to follow you and to see a halo in everyone because I haven't covered every angel in this book.

We don't know an exact number, but there are "innumerable angels"

Kate - housemixblog.com - What does the bible say about angels? April 23,2020

"But you have come to Mount Zion, to the city of the living God, the heavenly Jerusalem. You have come to thousands upon thousands of angels in joyful assembly"

The mountain of fear and the mountain of Joy

Hebrews 22:12

May you be guided, followed, excited and receive signs like I have in this book as confirmation that you're on the right path you're doing the right thing and you never have to worry about anything again for once you realise this you are having your own protected awakening.

Notes:

Notes:

Notes:

Notes:

Notes:

Printed in Great Britain
by Amazon